DEDICATION

To the Men and Women of Law Enforcement:
Stay resilient, stay focused, and stay well. For those at the
beginning of your career, stay focused. For those at the
midpoint, stay resilient. For those at the end, stay well.
And, for all stages of your career, whether
beginning, middle, or end—a heartfelt thank you for
your service. We need you more than ever before.

BODY
MIND
&
BADGE

STRATEGIES FOR NAVIGATING TRAUMA
& RESILIENCE IN LAW ENFORCEMENT

KATHRYN HAMEL, PhD

WITH CONTRIBUTIONS FROM:

CHIEF MIKE HAMEL (RET.)

HEATHER WILLIAMS, PsyD

OFFICER JOHN D. DARBY (RET.)

CHIEF CHARLES CELANO (RET.)

OFFICER ALEX MENDOZA

Body, Mind, and Badge: Strategies for Navigating Trauma and Resilience in Law Enforcement

www.kathrynhamelphd.com

Publisher

Made to Change the World Publishing
Nashville, TN
United States of America

Cover and interior design by Chelsea Jewell

Printed in the USA, Canada, and Europe

TABLE OF CONTENTS

FOREWORD

What stresses or traumas—vicarious or direct as a result of a critical incident—have you faced in your enforcement career? Do you feel like you handled them well? If not, what support systems—personal and organizational—could have helped? These are tough questions. Do they bring up feelings of discomfort? Stress? Perhaps even resentment, or at least wishes that you had more information about navigating the pitfalls of law enforcement at the start of your career?

Over the last couple of decades, the law enforcement community has made strides in recognizing the toll the career takes on officers. We are finally acknowledging the mental and emotional toll in particular. We've shined a light on how stresses and traumas, in the absence of support, negatively impact law enforcement officers, their colleagues, their families, and the communities that they serve. Consequently, we've begun to pay more attention to strategies and approaches to mitigate the negative impacts and bolster resiliency.

So, how do we cultivate mental health and resiliency at the individual *and* organization levels?

Dr. Kathryn Hamel knows how. Dr. Hamel is the ideal person to tackle this topic: she's a 25-year law enforcement veteran who earned a PhD in Public Safety Leadership. Her personal journey and resulting passion for finding and encouraging adaptive coping mechanisms for optimal mental health drove her research on physical fitness as a potential critical incident mitigation factor—the basis of her doctoral dissertation. But Dr. Hamel isn't interested in scholarship in a vacuum.

And that brings me to the beauty of *Body, Mind, and Badge: Strategies for Navigating Trauma and Resilience in Law Enforcement*. In this book, Dr. Hamel and several of her fellow law enforcement thought leaders provide paths to mental wellness based not only on scholarship, but also on personal experience. Yes, *Body, Mind, and Badge* includes plenty of scholarship that explains the wear and tear of trauma, the benefits of resiliency, and how wellness programs can best provide strategies for mental wellness. But it also includes law enforcement officers' personal journeys to wellness. The collective wisdom from these officers provides insight and demonstrates through their stories how physical, emotional, and mental healing are all *dependent on each other*.

Significantly, *Body, Mind, and Badge* examines the nexus between physical health and mental health. Of course, both are individually critical to comprehensive wellness, but they are also interconnected. Recognizing this, as Dr. Hamel does, is to our advantage. Law enforcement officers who focus on both thrive as each element strengthens the other. And the stories in this book compellingly illustrate the success of pursuing the mental and physical paths to health jointly. Such interconnectedness also underlies the importance of addressing both components if wellness programs are to be truly comprehensive.

As a 20-year chief of police, I encourage all law enforcement officers to read *Body, Mind, and Badge.* The strategies offered will help you navigate your own challenges and discern your paths to optimal mental health through physical fitness and resiliency, and encourage implementation of comprehensive physical and mental wellness programs—a priority of the International Association of Chiefs of Police. It is critical that law enforcement and municipal leaders institute these programs that help law enforcement officers maintain their health and wellness. It's to everyone's benefit.

We often commend you—the law enforcement officers who everyday risk their physical, emotional, and mental health. Let's manifest that appreciation and support you with the programs that will make and keep you your most healthy and resilient selves. We want you to not merely survive, but thrive in your career and your life. You deserve it.

DWIGHT HENNINGER
Chief of Police, Colorado, USA

ACKNOWLEDGMENTS

First, and foremost, I want to thank those that made this journey possible. I am eternally grateful for the guidance, love, and support of my husband, Mike Hamel, who continues to be the most important person in my life; thank you for your love and understanding. I am better for his influence in my life, and this book would not have been possible without his unending encouragement and support.

Every person, every story, and every interaction has a definitive impact on each one of us, whether this impact is growth through adversity, challenge, or triumph. I want to thank everyone who has been a part of my story. Thank you for the lessons, whether intentional or unintentional, and know that I am grateful to each of you for the influence you have had on my story and my journey.

A special thank you to the Hecht Trauma Institute and its founder, Dr. Gwen Hecht. Your support of this book is greatly appreciated. I am deeply grateful for your presence in my life, your advice, and your guidance throughout this process. Thank you for entrusting me to lead the Hecht Trauma Institute—I am honored to be a part of this organization and its work with first responders in *Cultivating Resilience in Law Enforcement*.

And a special thank you to the men and women who have dedicated their lives to the law enforcement profession. You are truly resilient individuals.

INTRODUCTION

At the beginning of my law enforcement career, I thought I was going to change the world. However, I quickly learned this would not be the case. The years of racing to crimes in progress, death notifications, and responding to critical incidents, suicides, and the worst days of peoples' lives have made an indelible impact on me. This impact is what I now know as vicarious trauma. And what did I learn? I learned that slowly, and over the years, the career changed me— for the better in some ways, not in others. Undoubtedly, I came out on the other side of it, nearly 25 years later, a very different person from my optimistic 20-something-year-old self.

This book is for all of you in law enforcement regardless of what stage you are in—to help you stay committed, stay engaged, stay resilient, and, most of all, be present. I commend the new recruits—soon to be officers or deputies—as well as current officers and deputies for their optimism. Don't lose this positivity. The job, while it will take its toll, must be a conscious choice that you make each and every day.

We all went into the career for the same reasons—to make a difference and yes, change the world. Remember those days of eager, fresh-faced, wide-eyed recruit mentality? The days that you would do the job for free! Those days before the "other days" crept in … the days that you did not make enough to endure another moment as a law enforcement officer. Dig deep during the "other days." As with all things, they will end, and you will come out on the other side of it. You may not come out the same version of yourself, but you will come out of it; this I assure you.

Deep down, I am compelled to share some of the changes that will likely occur as you navigate your law enforcement career. As a profession, law enforcement does not teach emotional survival. Do any of you recall a learning domain or knowledge domain on social emotional intelligence or emotional survival? It is not learned in the academy; it is learned on the job. Who are you learning this from? How did they learn it? Are they processing their own trauma effectively, or have they developed maladaptive coping skills, i.e., drinking, substance abuse, gambling, poor relationship choices, unhealthy eating, disordered sleeping patterns? This is not ideal, and as a profession we need to be better because you are owed better.

The purpose of this book is to provide you, whether you are in law enforcement or the loved one that supports someone in law enforcement, with effective strategies and a road map for not just surviving, but thriving, in a career in law enforcement. The book focuses on two imperative components of law enforcement wellness: physical fitness and resiliency. Cultivating both will enable you to mitigate the physical, mental, and emotional wear and tear that result from challenges of law enforcement. They will allow you to cope with the stress and trauma of critical incidents, in particular, and come out on the other side of the event a more resilient version of yourself.

Part One covers my time doing shift work and resulting

personal journey to physical fitness. It also discusses research on the unique health issues of law enforcement personnel, the pervasiveness of stress in the field, and the importance of physical fitness as a mitigating factor. This more academic research underlies my utmost belief that physical fitness programs must be integrated—somehow—into law enforcement organizations to support psychological wellness of law enforcement personnel.

Also included in Part One is the cautionary story of unexpected and devastating injury as a young, fit officer by Chief Mike Hamel (Ret.). He includes his assessment of the functional movement screen/predictive injury test and how he successfully brought it to the Irvine PD as part of an overall fitness program to help prevent the physical, emotional, and economic costs of injuries to law enforcement personnel. Chief Hamel encourages all supervisors and city staff to consider managing a fitness and wellness program for all departmental personnel.

In Part Two, Heather Williams, PsyD, discusses resiliency: what it is, why it's important for countering critical incidents, and how law enforcement personnel can integrate it into their lives. She proposes that law enforcement management help personnel build resilience by incorporating support systems into their organizations and by teaching inoculation training, hardiness training, psychoeducation, and cognitive-behavioral techniques like mindfulness. She also offers methods for individuals to build their own resiliency.

And in Part Three, retired and current police officers share their personal journeys to physical, mental, and emotional health and well-being. Officer John Darby (Ret.) and Chief Charles Celano (Ret.) relate how injury and illness, respectively, forced them into unexpected retirement. They share the methods they used to heal themselves physically and also how they overcame the shock and resulting sorrow of careers cut short. They emphasize that their insights on wellness are not just for retirees, but for current members of law enforcement. And Officer Alex Mendoza, a nutritionist, Reiki II practitioner, health coach, and mindfulness teacher, shares numerous emotional and physical paths to wellness, a final reminder that physical fitness and resiliency will allow you to not just survive, but thrive, in your law enforcement career.

Thank you for choosing such an important job, and for supporting law enforcement everywhere. They need your support more than ever before.

PART ONE

"Hey! You're Gonna Go Through a Whole Change in Your Entire Life"
Insights for Navigating Shift Work

KATHRYN HAMEL, PhD

Shift work. Typically, your life as a law enforcement officer consists of shift work for the first ten years.

Do you understand the difficulties that you'll face in your social life? Will you have a social life? How many parties, gatherings, graduations, holidays, and other events will you miss?

Do you know how much overtime you'll work and how much time you'll spend in court after your shift is over?

Do you know that shift work will disrupt your sleep—specifically your circadian rhythm—and cause long-lasting impacts on your physical health?

Do you know a health-positive approach to food and nutrition while handling shift work?

Do you have a physical fitness regimen as a means of

maintaining physical, mental, and emotional health during this time?

Do you know how important that is?

These are the questions that I didn't know I so desperately needed answered early in my law enforcement career. Through my personal experiences, as well as studying nutrition, fitness, and resiliency, I eventually found my own adaptive coping mechanisms. These answers did not come easily, and I wish I would have known them sooner! Nevertheless, my journey has helped me cultivate health and resiliency on an individual level. And, in my roles as an agency leader and scholar, I continue to delve deeper and advocate for the implementation of wellness programs, physical fitness, and resiliency programs at the organization level.

But, until we get there, I will help to answer these questions. Perhaps some (hopefully not all!) of my challenges from early on will sound familiar to you. Whatever challenges you face, I want you to read this book, find some insights that resonate, have that "a-ha" moment, and be able to say, "This is my plan to move forward."

My Journey Through Shift Work

I enrolled in the police academy in the Summer of 1994. A few months after starting, I got hired at a medium-sized police department. I poured myself into my work to prove that I was worthy to be there, to be in the room, to be in the conversation. While it was the 21st century, women in law enforcement were still not "accepted" during this time.

Exacerbating the stress of being a woman in law enforcement was the loss of my social support. I spent the decade that I was in the social prime of life working the graveyard shift. And, sure enough, I faced difficulties in socializing. I didn't see my friends and family who were at home, relaxing, and enjoying their nights and weekends. Because I always had to say "no" to activities, my friends stopped calling. And that's where the "us against them" started for me. Shift work limited my network to other first responders. "No one understands us. Other first responders are the only group of people who get me." Sound familiar?

In addition to shift work, I, like all young officers, worked a lot of overtime. And when I wasn't working overtime, I was in court. During my typical routine on the night shift, I worked from 5:30 p.m. to 6:00 a.m. If I was lucky, I left work at 6:00 a.m. But on court days, I slept in my car for 30–45 minutes before heading to the locker room for a shower. By 8:00 a.m., I was in court, where I'd often remain until 5:00 p.m., or the courtroom closed for the day. Then I'd go back to work and report for my shift at 5:30 p.m.

Sometimes I didn't sleep at all for days on end. As a detective, I once worked a Special Victims case trying to find a missing girl and, because of the urgency, I didn't go home to sleep for 36 hours. I was often so sleep deprived that I started seeing things dashing in front of my car that weren't actually there! If you too have seen things jump in front of your car while driving or have fallen asleep at a red light, then you know that sleep deprivation often emulates the effects of being under the influence.

And that is dangerous. According to Vila (2009), being awake for 19 hours is the equivalent of having a 0.05 blood alcohol content (BAC). And being awake for 24 hours is equal to a 0.10 BAC. This is at, or in some states over, the legal limit for a DUI conviction, according to the National Highway Traffic Safety Administration (NHTSA 2015). Driving while sleep deprived is especially concerning for police officers who are often forced to work long hours and who may be called upon to make split-second life and death decisions.

According to Samuels (2009), shift work impacts sleep patterns, disrupts the circadian rhythm, and can cause a decrease in performance. It is also well documented that the older we get, the more we are impacted by sleep deprivation (Vila 2009). Furthermore, sleep deprivation can influence spatial orientation, slow reaction times, increase hunger, decrease cognitive processes like reasoning, and increase the risk of heart disease. It is estimated that more than half of all police officers don't get enough sleep, and 40 percent have reported falling asleep while driving (Vila 2009).

Even when I was at home, sleep eluded me. I bought every drape, over-the-counter sleep aid, gadget, and device available on the market to help me sleep. Despite the blackout drapes that decreased the daylight in the bedroom, the alarm clock that emitted sounds of nature, and the sleep aids, I still couldn't sleep because the world kept going on around me. The kids played, the gardeners worked, the trash truck picked up, or a package that required a signature arrived. At one point, I'd bought a new home and the house behind me was under construction for six months. There were times I would lay in bed and just cry. I was so physically, mentally, and emotionally exhausted because I couldn't sleep. I even tried to sleep in my closet. It was quiet, insulated, and darkened, but only sometimes did I succeed. And then, it was back to work an hour or two later, and the cycle continued.

Not only was the sleep deprivation itself unhealthy, but it fed into my desire for quick comfort food. Do you feel hungry when you're tired? I sure did. During this time, I met a nice man, we began dating, and married six months later. Newly married, children were definitely something that the two of us wanted—my then husband was the last of his line and having children was important to him. But we struggled with fertility, eventually turning to fertility treatments. Enter days of needles, blood tests, poking, prodding, surgery, and pain. Here too I turned to food for comfort. Hormone injections and steroid medications had me ravenous at every turn and I ate whatever I could as often as I could, including an XL cheese pizza by myself one night!

Between fertility treatments and shift work, I ultimately gained nearly 60 pounds. My once svelte, 140-pound body grew until I topped the scales at 200 pounds, which was very unhealthy for my height and frame. My size 4 uniform pants grew to a size 16. Add to that weight another 30 pounds of police gear, bullet proof vest, and boots, and, at my heaviest in full uniform, I tipped the scales at nearly 230 pounds. As a 5' 6" female, this was incredibly hard on my body.

As police work deals with sudden events that require immediate action or physical response, this precluded me from performing at my peak, and, thus, added to my stress. It also stressed out my potential partners. In fact, another female officer pulled me aside and said, "You're a complete disaster. Look at you. I wouldn't want to go on a call with you." She was right. I was like a turtle—how would I run and jump over a fence?! My knees hurt. I couldn't breathe going up the stairs. I had no chance in a fight.

Her indignation was warranted. One night, after indulging in my usual fast-food dinner of a bean burrito, my beat partner and I received a radio call of a shooting that had just occurred. We arrived on scene, made eye contact with the armed suspect, radioed for treatment of the victim, and began pursuing him on foot. The suspect ran through an alley, over obstacles, and into a parking lot. My partner and I eventually tackled him, and as I proceeded to hand-cuff him, I threw up bean burrito all over him. It certainly surprised the suspect, and any others nearby got a good laugh. While this was not my best moment, I appreciate it as it made me pause and reflect about my health, my ability to be safe, and my ability to keep my partners safe. At that point, I endeavored to be better, fitter, and healthier for my partners, my community, and myself.

That night, I ordered a treadmill and had it delivered to my home. Slowly and methodically, I began to walk more—taking my dog for longer walks to start—and vowed to change my diet. Soon after, I was walking on the treadmill for hours, night after night, while eating a diet of broccoli and white rice. While it wasn't the healthiest weight loss regimen, I quickly dropped 30 pounds and began a journey of lifelong fitness. I remained committed to my fitness journey, enrolled in a nutrition course, began resistance training, and returned to weight training, which had once been a love of mine as I was involved in competitive weightlifting during my high school days.

Fast forward to April 16, 2000. I was working out nearly every day with a trainer, had dropped over 30 pounds, and was lean and fit. In the early morning hours of that day, I was working a solo assignment on patrol when I found myself near a call of a felony stolen vehicle that had just occurred. I, along with the primary officer, quickly responded to the area and located the suspect vehicle. A high-speed vehicle pursuit ensued, and we traveled at upwards of 111 mph through the streets of Los Angeles as the suspect attempted to evade capture.

As we navigated these incredibly high speeds, I was uber focused on the suspect and began to develop a bit of tunnel vision. The suspect continued driving at a high rate of speed and drove toward an area of steep and windy roads with sharp hairpin turns. And, to complicate matters, it was 3:00 in the morning and had just started to drizzle, creating dangerous road conditions for high-speed pursuits along winding and hilly roadways.

The suspect continued at high speeds with us right up on his tail. Suddenly, he took a turn too quickly and bounced off a barrier while navigating a nearly 90-degree turn. I was still driving in excess of 100 mph, and as I slowed to navigate the same turn, I hit a slick of oil left by the suspect's damaged vehicle and began a fishtail spin from which I was unable to recover. My vehicle immediately decelerated as it struck the same barrier, bounced off a concrete pole, and came to a rest after colliding with barriers, poles, and a tree. As I lost control of my vehicle, my entire life flashed before my eyes. It's true what they say about "compressed life review." You take stock of your life when you believe that it is nearing its end.

I suffered from significant orthopedic injuries, including a dislocated knee, a separated shoulder, acute head trauma, and herniated disks in my neck and back, as well as major internal injuries, including a heart valve injury. I was hospitalized and then off work for nearly eight months to undergo physical therapy. As I continued with cardiac and orthopedic rehabilitation, my doctors shared with me that I may not have survived if I had not been as fit as I was. Specifically, one of the orthopedic doctors in charge of my care revealed that I would have likely broken my femur and hip (as opposed to injuring them) if my quad muscles had not been as developed as they were at the time of the collision.

My commitment to physical fitness likely saved my life, and it inspired my continued belief in and passion for fitness.

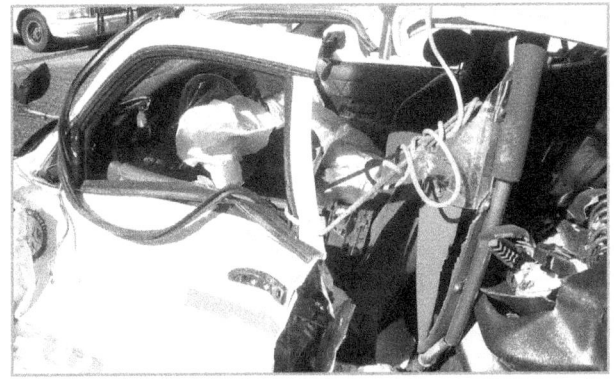

My Personal Fitness Practice

In addition to keeping my body healthy, I turn to physical fitness as a means of coping, handling stress, and self-regulation. This appeals to me because I can self-pace and need not rely on anyone other than myself to regulate.

I am committed to this practice by working out at least six days a week, and I try to eat healthy, including juicing on occasion as a meal replacement. In addition, at least two or more times a week, I meditate and take Barre, yoga, and/or Pilates classes. I also perform some sort of weight bearing exercise along with extended periods of cardiovascular exercise.

Taking the time to exercise has allowed me to self-regulate and has afforded me the opportunity to handle my stress in unique and positive ways. The advantages to physical fitness as my personal self-regulation practice have been two-fold: I quickly shed the additional weight and am slimmer and more fit than I have ever been, and I have the added confidence of being able to handle any sudden event that comes my way during the course and scope of my daily activities.

To calm the mind, I practice yogic breathing at random times during the day when the office—now house in today's remote work environment—is quiet. My yogic breathing encompasses the recommendations in *Practical Stress Management: A Comprehensive Workbook for Managing Change and Promoting Health*, and is completed in five steps. **Step One:** Kneel down or stand up straight. **Step Two:** Inhale slowly and completely. **Step Three:** Exhale air completely. **Step Four:** Gradually fill lungs completely. And **Step Five:** Repeat steps 2–4 five or six times.

Of course, fitness needs evolve. I've needed different things at different times throughout my career, and will continue to do so as I navigate post-law enforcement life.

Conclusion

I hope you realize that you are not alone in your challenges from shift work. Remember the questions posed at the beginning of this chapter? If you haven't already done so, ask yourself those important questions. As I wrote this chapter and reflected on my law enforcement journey, I wished someone would have asked me to consider them. Sometimes just anticipating the challenge that lies ahead helps to mitigate it. Next, read and take to heart the multitude of reflections and good advice offered throughout this book. The other contributors and I want this compilation to help you navigate your chosen profession with confidence, grace, and a whole lot of resilience. Take agency over your law enforcement career; there is much joy to be found in it and on the other side of it. My sincerest hope is that any one of these reflections or pieces of advice helps you cultivate fitness and resiliency techniques that will enable you to not only survive, but thrive, throughout your law enforcement career.

For more information about the stress inherent in law enforcement—from shift work to critical incidents—and the importance of physical fitness as a mitigating factor, I've shared an excerpt of my dissertation, "Impact of Physical Fitness on Law Enforcement Officer Stress and Coping Skills."

Impact of Physical Fitness on Law Enforcement Officer Stress and Coping Skills

KATHRYN HAMEL, PhD

The contemporary law enforcement officer must be able to perform feats unimaginable where super-human strength, resolve, and problem-solving skills are necessary to prevail and survive critical incidents. They respond to calls for service where they will be tested and must be of sound mind, and body, for the best possible outcomes. The work of police officers has been proven inherently dangerous and stressful (Regehr et al. 2008). How that stress manifests in each individual law enforcement officer may depend on several factors including the officer's level of physical fitness, their ability to manage stress, the support systems in place, their past involvement in a critical incident, and their level of coping skills they possess at the time of the event. From this perspective, focusing on physical fitness is a critical component for police managers to ensure law enforcement officers responsible for protecting our communities are poised to provide only the highest levels of service (Chae and Boyle 2012; Fiedler 2009; Morash et al. 2006).

Law Enforcement Is Inherently Stressful—Physically and Emotionally

Evidence suggests that law enforcement officers are at increased risk for certain physical ailments, including heart disease (Gerber et al. 2010; Violanti 2006), low-back injuries and other musculoskeletal injuries, and lung problems among others (Wall et al. 2009; Baughman et al. 2013). Incidents of law enforcement officers injured as a result of their inability to perform the functions of their assigned duties continue to rise (Tanogoshi et al. 2008).

Law enforcement officers who work night shift(s) are more prone to injury due to several factors including sleeplessness, fatigue, and a higher level of dangerous calls for service (Violanti et al. 2013). The lack of sleep and the disruption of the normal sleep cycles leads to decreased decision-making abilities after sustained periods of sleeplessness (Violanti et al. 2013).

Furthermore, these stressors, such as shift work and fatigue, increase the physiological stressors of the body, which leads to increased production of the stress-hormone cortisol (Wirth et al. 2011). Overall, members of the law enforcement population disproportionately suffer from the effects of stress and fatigue leading to life-threatening conditions such as metabolic disorders, cancer, melanoma, heart disease, and diabetes (Violanti 2006; Wirth et al. 2011).

Hence, law enforcement physical fitness and wellness programs have traditionally sought to address these physical ailments. But members of the law enforcement population are also at increased risk of psychological stressors that lead to depression and suicidal ideations (Galatzer-Levy et al. 2011; Harris 2009). Ensuring law enforcement officers are physically fit requires they be mentally fit, as well, in order to best serve their respective communities.

Police officers also are exposed to a variety of emotionally charged critical incidents, including crimes involving violence, exposure to dead bodies, and mass casualties. In addition, police shootings, traffic collisions, threats to their lives or the lives of their partners are highly charged situations that create a tremendous amount of stress (Becker et al. 2009). As a result of exposure to critical incidents and irregular work schedules, the police officer population suffers from increased mental and emotional stress and decreased coping skills (Fiedler 2009). Involvement in police shootings and high-speed traffic collisions contribute to police-specific stress such as peritraumatic dissociation and post-traumatic stress disorder (PTSD) (Novy 2012). PTSD affects many officers who witness traumatic incidents during the course of their work (Yuan et al. 2011; Galatzer-Levy et al. 2011; Gerber et al. 2010; Morash et al. 2006). Long-term exposure to untreated trauma may lead to maladaptive coping mechanisms (Halpern et al. 2009).

In a seminal work on stress and coping within the law enforcement population, Aaron (2000) measured stress and coping in a sampling of 42 law enforcement officers in Charlottesville, Virginia. Specifically, he measured three variables: stress, dissociation, and psychological adjustment. The independent variable was stress, while the dependent variables were psychological adjustment and dissociation. He found that law enforcement officers who were repeatedly exposed to stressors in the scope of their duties had correlating chronic stress, dissociation, and psychological adjustment. Aaron (2000) hypothesized that law enforcement officers who experience numerous stressors often dissociate as a coping mechanism, have memories of stressful events, and have difficulty adjusting, both on and off duty. Likewise, Galatzer-Levy et al. (2011) measured stress-related symptomology present in police officers exposed to life-threatening situations (or critical incidents) including those involved in shootings and those physically attacked while on duty. Galatzer-Levy et al. (2011) sampled 178 active-duty police officers from the states of California and New York. The findings of Galatzer-Levy et al. (2011) mirrored those of Aaron (2000).

Additionally, Aaron (2000) found a statistically significant difference in the coping skills of officers by gender. Morash et al. (2006), who conducted research on 947 individual police officers from 11 different police departments across the United States serving affluent and underserved communities alike, concluded that women and minorities experience the majority of workplace conflict that results in stress. Moreover, women and minority law enforcement officers are more inclined to feel unsupported by the agency responses to workplace conflict (Morash et al. 2006).

Additionally, Morash et al. (2006) concluded that law enforcement officers who are exposed to stressful encounters in the field often experience more stress associated with the agency's response to the encounter rather than the encounter itself.

Thirty years of research indicates that police officers are prone to physical health problems, mental stress, and psychological distress (Barling et al., 2005; Gilmartin, 2002). A law enforcement professional's stress literally involves making critical decisions in life and death situations (Barling et al., 2005). "The officer's journey, all too often, takes its toll—a toll in world view from positive to negative, from idealistic to cynical, from physically active and fit to sedentary and potentially unhealthy" (Gilmartin 2002, p. 5).

Mitigating Stress to Build Public Trust

As public servants, police officers are charged with safeguarding the public and building public trust. To be successful in this regard, law enforcement must be balanced, professional, and thoughtful in its approach. To this end, officers who have well-developed physical, mental, and emotional stress management skills and coping mechanisms are better prepared to carry out this mission. Indeed, when members of law enforcement perform at peak levels, they are more engaged and productive within the organization and are generally happier than those law enforcement officers that are sedentary and not physically fit. (Gerber et al. 2010; Lagestad 2011).

Moreover, officers who are better able to deal with stress, and those who have more sophisticated coping strategies, are better able to better serve the public (Fiedler, 2009). Those with untreated trauma could exhibit poor behaviors, poor performance, absenteeism, and performance issues, such as treating citizens with disrespect or using excessive force, which erode public trust (Galatzer-Levy et al. 2011; Gerber et al. 2010).

Officers who suffer from debilitating stressors are not as likely to serve their respective communities to the best of their abilities. Thus, managing stress and increasing coping skills is critical to the success of any law enforcement agency. Mitigating stress and enhancing coping skills sets for officers helps reduce aggression, while enhancing compassion and patience when they interact with members of the public (Violanti et al. 2011).

When law enforcement officers are better able to service their communities, perceptions of the police agencies are bolstered in the minds of the residents.

Physical Fitness as Mitigation Factor

There have been many studies demonstrating the physical benefits of physical fitness in the general population (Gerber et al. 2010; Parks and Steelman 2008; Regehr et al. 2008; Quigley 2008). Physical fitness as it pertains to the law enforcement population requires that an individual law enforcement officer be of sound body and mind in order to perform at peak levels. Individual law enforcement officers who engage in a physical fitness routine are better prepared for the inherent challenges of policing function (Kasper 2010; Dugdill et al. 2009) and better able to perform the required job skills and tasks such as running, jumping, crawling, sustained foot pursuit of a suspect, and use of physical force against another (Collingwood et al. 2004; Quigley 2008). Moreover, during a shift, a law enforcement officer could drive for miles, respond to numerous calls for service that do not require physical strength, and then, suddenly, be in the fight for his or her life. For this reason, the law enforcement officer must be prepared physically for the trials and tribulations of the policing function (Dugdill et al. 2009).

Due to the long hours (shift work) and strenuous work of a law enforcement officer, physical fitness remains crucial to overall health and wellness (Baughman et al. 2013). Comprehensive wellness programs for public safety personnel should include cardiovascular wellness dimensions, which target modifiable risk factors (Gerber et al. 2010; Smith and Tooker 2008). As physical fitness is so closely linked to cardiovascular fitness, strategies such as regular workouts mitigate future cardiovascular problems. The cost of an in-service heart attack for a police officer ranges between $400,000 and $750,000 (Bullock, n.d.). Promoting physical fitness within the law enforcement population mitigates incidents of chronic stress and reduces the overall risk of injury, illness, and even death.

Physical fitness not only prepares your body for the demands of the job, but also reduces stress from the job (Dugdill et al. 2009; Johnson 2009; Lagestad 2012). For example, a 2010 study of Swiss police officers and first responders studied the buffering effects of physical exercise in 533 Swiss first responders (Gerber et al. 2010). The authors found that officers with increased stress had poorer health, while those in better health with lower stress utilized fitness and exercise. The researchers concluded that exercise protects against stress-related health problems and helps foster a healthy and productive workforce, one better capable to cope with chronic stress specific to the law enforcement population (Gerber et al. 2010).

Likewise, organizations that implement physical fitness and wellness programs experience decreases in employee absenteeism and work-related injuries over time (Benavides and David 2010; Gerber et al. 2010; Regehr et al. 2008). In fact, Benavides and David (2010) report that healthy employees are more productive and their levels of absenteeism amongst the workforce are greatly reduced. Moreover, these programs reduce agency liability (Quigley 2008). Physical exercise has been touted as an individually-targeted intervention strategy *and* an organizational intervention strategy. Barling et al. (2005, p. 615) posit, "exercise strengthens the vital organs to allow the body to withstand higher levels of stress," which may, in turn, make the employee considerably more productive.

However, overall, as a profession, law enforcement has not performed exceptionally well in the area of implementing and sustaining physical and psychological wellness programs, despite evidence that such programs are beneficial (Benavides and David 2010; Kasper 2010). For the vast majority of law enforcement agencies, there is not a physical fitness standard one must achieve or maintain post-academy (Johnson 2009; Kasper 2010). While some agencies offer incentives for participation in various forms of physical fitness programs, for most, there is no negative consequence for not participating (Johnson 2009). Other agencies, though they might wish for structured workplace physical fitness and wellness programs, lack the necessary funding (a challenge as public funds are used) (Kasper 2010; Tanigoshi et al. 2008).

Additionally, the culture of public safety organizations may present barriers to the implementation of programs designed to enhance psychological wellness (Halpern et al. 2008). In a study of 60 emergency medical technicians from a major urban area, researchers concluded these employees would welcome emotional support in the form of a critical incident debriefing following a traumatic event; however, they also found barriers that interfere with successful intervention programs, including stigma of appearing weak and inadequate training to initiate or lead critical incident debriefings (Halpern et al. 2008).

Nevertheless, public safety leaders must seek to break these barriers. As physical fitness for law enforcement officers is positively correlated with enhanced stress management and coping skills, it can provide law enforcement executives one more strategy to help these employees mitigate the physical, mental, and psychological impacts of traumatic events they will inevitably experience.

Conclusion

The responsibilities of law enforcement officers are complex, taxing, and often involve life and death situations and scenarios. Law enforcement executives have the very important responsibility of identifying, recruiting, hiring, and training individuals who will be charged to serve our communities professionally, ethically, and competently. It is important to remember officers are hired from the human race; they are fallible, often fragile, impressionable, and shaped by their experiences. While many of their experiences drive them toward a career in law enforcement and prepare them for this role, it is important to remember that law enforcement officers continue to be impacted by new experiences after they are hired and throughout their careers. These often involve witnessing trauma, tragedy, and crisis up close and personal, and undoubtedly shape their outlook, psyche, and perspective. Physical fitness programs to aid in stress management and coping skills are a commodity for many who dedicate their lives to the law enforcement profession.

I believe that we can improve outcomes so that our law enforcement officers live longer, happier, and healthier lives.

ABOUT KATHRYN HAMEL, PhD

Dr. Kathryn Hamel, PhD, is the Chief Executive Officer of the Hecht Trauma Institute.

Dr. Hamel served the southern California communities for nearly 25 years as a law enforcement professional for two midsize police departments. During her law enforcement career, she earned the rank of Lieutenant. Her experience in leadership, personnel, training, homeland security, criminal investigations, supervision, and management earned the respect of her peers and subordinates—no small feat in a male-dominated field.

Preparing for a post-law enforcement career, Dr. Hamel earned a doctorate while working full-time shift work. Upon retirement from law enforcement, she entered academia as the Dean of the School of Criminal Justice and Criminology at a local university. Her advanced leadership knowledge and skills earned her a promotion to Vice President of Human Resources with an added benefit of crafting individual professional development plans.

Building upon this success, she was next promoted to Senior Vice President of Human Resources and Organizational Development. And now, as the Chief Executive Officer of the Hecht Trauma Institute, she continues to mentor and empower her staff, as she enhances and enriches its Servant Leadership culture.

A committed community volunteer, Dr. Hamel has almost three decades of experience in guiding charitable organizations and is currently a board member of KinderVision, a nonprofit co-founded by her late mother, Ashby Sebastian. She is the Hecht Trauma Institute's nominee for the Irvine Chamber of Commerce's *"2020 Women of Influence"* and *"Executive of the Year."*

Dr. Hamel earned a Doctor of Philosophy in Public Safety Leadership from Capella University, a Master's degree in Criminal Justice from Chapman University, and a Bachelor's degree in Occupational Studies from California State University/Long Beach.

Don't Get Stuck: How to Avoid Injury in Law Enforcement

CHIEF MIKE HAMEL (RET.)

Growing up, I was always a pretty good athlete. I started playing ice hockey at four years old and was quite a successful hockey player. In high school, I added track and became a track star. While I knew that I was lucky to have physical skills, it was nevertheless something I always took for granted. Physicality came naturally to me in my teens and twenties simply because I was young. I never worried about conditioning, stretching, or actually maintaining my physical health.

I entered law enforcement with the LAPD in 1993. In 1995, I moved to the Irvine PD. I remember watching a particular training video where Sergeant Rhonda Wood demonstrated the proper way to get in and out of a car to avoid hurting one's back. She opened her car door, turned around, sat on the edge of her seat so that her legs were outside of the car with her feet on the ground, and then she very methodically moved one leg into the car and then the other leg into the car. At the time, it seemed pretty silly. I thought, "Who gets in a car that way? It's impractical. And I don't have back issues … I'm never going to … my back is fine."

By 1998, not only was I an active young cop, I also was playing hockey with the Orange County Gunslingers. I was 28 years old and on top of the world. I was fit and active. I didn't heed the warnings about how common back injuries were among law enforcement personnel. The weight of gun belts on the hips, combined with the constant entering and exiting of cars, and running while chasing suspects takes a toll on many parts of the body, but especially the lower back. By this time, I'd been wearing a gun belt for five years. I started to have an inkling of pain in my lower back, but nothing concerning.

But, during one Gunslingers game, I made a quick turn while skating, and, suddenly, my lower back erupted in excruciating pain. I went down on the ice. I couldn't move. The pain was unbearable, like nothing I'd ever experienced. Eventually, I got to my feet, but the pain in my lower back was debilitating. I couldn't play hockey.

I could barely work. I had to move so tenuously and be so very careful that work became cumbersome. Turns out, an MRI showed that I had a two-millimeter disk protrusion in the L5-S1 joint. It wasn't enough for surgery, so the orthopedist prescribed physical therapy. I went to physical therapy for many, many months trying to work through this injury while still being a cop and doing my job. But the injury consumed me. It was the first thing I would think about when I got out of bed—my lack of flexibility and ease of movement at work. And I thought about how I couldn't play hockey anymore, which depressed me. Hockey was my outlet, something I'd played for so long that its loss was like losing a best friend. I also grieved the loss of not being able to do the things I wanted to do. And I began to wonder about the impact that my career had on my body; how it might have led to that injury.

After the denial and then the depression, I finally started to wrap my head around the injury and its larger consequences on my life. I more deeply understood that I wouldn't be able to exactly do the things I did before; that I wouldn't be the same again. One of the watershed moments in this whole journey was when I said to my physical therapist, "Hey, tell me how long do I need to go to physical therapy; how long do I need to do these exercises that you're telling me I need to do three days a week?" And the answer was, "Well, for the rest of your life."

So, for many, many, many years, I religiously stretched and did my physical therapy exercises. At first, I had to fight through the pain. But, as the muscles strengthened over time, the pain went away. It got to the point where if I *didn't* do the exercises, then I had pain. Eventually, I started playing a little bit of hockey again. It wasn't the same. I have really tight hip flexors and poor flexibility; of course, being 51 now might also be a culprit. Early on, I asked my orthopedist if I'd ever need surgery. He responded, "Well not right now, but one day you will."

Fast-forward almost 25 years, and I have not had surgery. I have not needed surgery; I don't have any pain. Occasionally, my back feels sore. Sometimes, if I lay on my back too long, I get kind of numb in my leg. But, through perseverance, a lot of physical therapy, and really trying to heal and take care of my back, I'm able to work. And, ironically, every time I get into a police car now, I do so the way I was trained to do in the '90s when I thought it was a big joke. I'm a living lesson in why you must take care of yourself when you are younger.

Now I'm determined to share my experience in order to help current and future law enforcement officers avoid injuries. When I was deputy chief, I brought a fitness program to Irvine PD that was sponsored through Santa Ana College. Today, it is still going full force. It's completely sponsored by the department, by the city. We have both officers and professional staff who work in the field that sign up every year. The fitness program utilizes a predictive injury test/functional movement screen, which is designed to identify biomechanical weaknesses and then dictate prescriptive exercises to help enhance flexibility and strength, and, therefore, reduce the likelihood of injury. The program also involves a stress treadmill; a strength test; and a blood test—a full wellness picture. And it's free. Many of our personnel have embraced the fitness program. Though we're still evaluating empirical evidence to see if it actually saves money or reduces injuries, anecdotally, the value can't be overstated. It's been quite remarkable for our personnel. My hope is that the program has helped our participating younger officers ward off or prevent injuries like mine.

So, remember, just because you're young and feel invincible, really listen to people that have been there/ done that, and realize that you have to preserve yourself. This profession is a marathon, not a sprint. Likewise, senior managers and senior people in law enforcement ought to give back, educate, and share our experiences with younger officers, so that they avoid the harmful attitudes of believing they're invincible and don't need to take care of their bodies. Especially now, with retirement coming at 57 instead of 50, it's even more imperative that people take care of their bodies in this profession so that they can retire without ailments and live pain-free down the road.

For more information about the revolutionary predictive injury testing programs, I've shared my research and experiences in "Predictive Injury Testing, Biomechanics, and Corrective Exercise: One Component of Officer Wellness" (reprinted and updated from original © 2013 California Commission on Peace Officer Standards and Training).

Predictive Injury Testing, Biomechanics, and Corrective Exercise: One Component of Officer Wellness

CHIEF MIKE HAMEL (RET.)

January 18, 2013: I'm meeting Captain Mike Contreras at 8:30 a.m. at the front doors of the Irvine Police Department. He's dressed in workout gear, carrying a gym bag and a couple of interesting props. I see a PVC pipe and an object resembling a 2" x 6" with large measurement markings on its face—like a giant ruler. I had spoken to him on the phone after learning he was the Orange County Fire Authority's fitness expert, but today we're meeting for the first time. Contreras has agreed to assist me in my quest to enhance the level of overall wellness and job satisfaction for the 205 sworn officers at the Irvine Police Department. His specific expertise is how to approach wellness scientifically.

As I escort him upstairs, he tells me more about the Functional Movement Screen™ (FMS). "The FMS™ is a predictive injury tool, and we are using it to identify our recruits who are most at risk to injure themselves in the line of duty or during training," he says. "The real value," he continues, "is someone trained to administer FMS™ can use the results to prescribe corrective exercises designed to correct faulty movement patterns." Mike concludes his introduction to the FMS™ by noting some studies suggest individuals who overcome their deficiencies may decrease their propensity for musculoskeletal injury under a variety of conditions (O'Connor et al. 2012; Bates et al. 2007; Contreras 2010).

As we reach the city's wellness center inside City Hall, Contreras sets up all of his contraptions. "I'm going to put you through a series of seven tests designed to evaluate your functional movement. I'll assign a score between one and three for each test. The sum of the scores for these tests will be your overall score."

As I align my feet with my shoulders, I squat while bracing a PVC pipe with my arms extended over my head. During the next 15 minutes, Contreras watches my form while I bend, balance, reach, and lunge. He takes measurements and makes notes. When I have completed all seven movements that comprise the screen, he announces that in a range from 0 to 21, I scored an overall 9. "Is that good or bad?" I inquire. "It's not good," he responds. A lower FMS™ score is correlated with poorer movement patterns. According to Contreras, if I were an Orange County Fire Authority recruit, I wouldn't be permitted to "workout" in the traditional sense of the word. Instead, a cadre of corrective exercises designed to restore my functional movement would be prescribed. Since a part of my goal for the day is to assess how working cops might use the FMS™, I wondered to myself what score we would use. First, though, I had to get a better understanding of the FMS™ and how predictive injury testing actually works.

Predictive Injury Testing

The FMS™ was developed by Gray Cook, a board-certified orthopedic clinical specialist, and Lee Burton, who holds a PhD in Health Promotion and Wellness. Originally introduced in 1998 to rate and rank the movement patterns of high school athletes, the FMS™ today has been applied in many other settings (Cook et al. 2012). According to the creators, the validity of the tool in predicting injuries stems from the test's ability to identify "weaknesses, imbalances, asymmetries and limitations" that cause compensatory movement patterns, which lead to poor biomechanics and possible future musculoskeletal injury (Cook et al. 2012, p. 1). The FMS™ reflects an appreciation of the human body as a kinetic chain consisting of interdependent joints and muscles working together to create functional movement (Schneiders et al. 2011). FMS™ technology already has been adopted by a growing number of governmental organizations, such as the Orange County Fire Authority, the United States Secret Service, and various branches of the United States Military. According to the Functional Movement Systems website, many college football programs and nearly all NFL teams also successfully use the FMS™ to assess athletes and their propensity for injury.

While perhaps the most prominent, the FMS™ is not the only predictive injury test. Among many others, the Star Excursion Balance Test (SEBT) and general joint laxity tests have been accepted as screening tools to identify athletes who are at greater risk for lower extremity injury (Filipa et al. 2010; Benjaminse et al. 2012). Other companies, such as UK-based Intelligent Training Systems™ (ITS), also promote predictive injury testing through an assessment of intrinsic biomechanics to identify biomechanical flaws, asymmetries, and imbalances that give rise to prescriptive corrective exercises (Langston 2013).

ITS™ worked with many police and fire departments in the past, including the South Yorkshire Police Department in the UK. According to Danny Langston of ITS, while official research data is not available, initial assessments indicate the ITS™ system is effective in reducing injuries among South Yorkshire police officers.

Functional Movement Screening in the Fire Service

The Orange County Fire Authority has used the FMS™ in its fire academy since 2007 to identify recruits most at risk for musculoskeletal injury. In a preliminary study of recruits in two academy classes, those who scored 14 or less on the FMS™ were twice as likely to be injured during the academy. And, in further study, 113 recruits from four consecutive fire academies were screened using the FMS™. Although only 47 percent of the recruits scored 14 or less, this group accounted for 72 percent of the total musculoskeletal injuries reported during the academy and 85 percent of the total cost to treat these injuries (Contreras 2010).

One study in the Tucson, Arizona Fire Department (Tucson Firefighter Study) has already demonstrated appropriate post-FMS™ intervention strategies can be beneficial. In this study of 433 firefighters, the prescribed corrective exercise routines and accompanying training to promote optimal body mechanics reduced lost time by 62 percent, and the overall number of injuries by 42 percent over a year's period, compared to a historical control group (Bates et al. 2007).

Predictive Injury Testing in Law Enforcement?

While the job duties of a firefighter and police officer differ, the movements required to perform specific job tasks are similar. Because of these similarities, the prospect of similar success with predictive injury screening in law enforcement is promising. Contreras reports the top three musculoskeletal injuries within the Orange County Fire Authority are back, knee, and shoulder injuries—all relatively equal in distribution (Contreras 2013). A recent analysis of workers' compensation claims from 2008 through 2012 for the Irvine Police Department revealed musculoskeletal injury data that mirrored the Orange County Fire Authority's data. The fact that many back, knee, and shoulder injuries are due to repetitive use further supports a similarity between the movement patterns of police officers and firefighters.

Exercise physiologist Kari Mefferd, who directs Anaheim Police Department's wellness program, and Hayley Stevens, Glendale Police Department's wellness coordinator, have incorporated the FMS™ into their agencies' respective comprehensive wellness programs (Mefferd 2013; Stevens 2013). Both agree the FMS™ is one useful tool in identifying police officers who may be at risk for injury. Mefferd, who is certified to administer the FMS™, advocates follow-up with a physical therapist for any FMS™ participant who reports pain during the screening.

Both Mefferd and Stevens have worked in partnership with exercise physiologist Terri Wann, who is the coordinator for Santa Ana College's wellness program. Santa Ana College has offered comprehensive fitness evaluations to public safety personnel for the past 35+ years, and the FMS™ is one component of their overall program. Wann explains the FMS™ is an effective screening tool since public safety personnel are often athletic and fit, but some possess poor body mechanics (Wann 2013). Santa Ana College's clients include 22 fire departments and four police departments, including Glendale and Anaheim. Wann has collected FMS™ data on thousands of public safety personnel, but this data has not been analyzed.

Incorporating Predictive Injury Testing
Into Wellness Programming

Law enforcement leaders have good cause to take action to mitigate their personnel's potential for job-related injuries. In Tucson, between 2002 and 2008, injuries to public safety personnel cost the city 20 million dollars, and the injury rate for these personnel was more than two times the state average (Brosseau 2008). And in one Orange County city, 83 percent of the open workers' compensation claims were linked to police officers or firefighters (Cassidy 2011). The research, as reviewed here, clearly supports predictive injury testing for police officers as a viable solution for agencies wishing to mitigate future injury to their personnel while enhancing their health and job performance.

Injury Prevention Training Should Augment
Predictive Injury Testing

It is important to distinguish between predictive injury screening and injury prevention programs. A corrective exercise program flowing from a predictive injury screen can reduce the likelihood of injury *when* movement occurs, whereas an injury prevention program teaches *how* to move to mitigate injury potential. Thus, predictive injury testing and injury prevention programming work in synergy to reduce the likelihood of line-of-duty and training injuries.

As suggested in the Tucson Firefighter Study, the value of injury prevention programming for recruits and in-service officers should not be overlooked. The Tucson firefighters participating in the study not only received prescriptions for corrective exercise to strengthen and stabilize their core, they also received comprehensive training related to proper posture and biomechanical form when engaging in physical activities involving pushing, pulling, twisting, or lifting (Bates et al. 2007).

Predictive Injury Testing and Corrective Exercise as One Aspect of Comprehensive Wellness

Mefferd, Stevens, and Wann stress to law enforcement administrators that predictive injury testing and corrective exercise is only one component of a comprehensive wellness program. Comprehensive wellness encompasses *any program administered through a city or a police department for sworn personnel, whether mandatory or voluntary in nature, and irrespective of compensation or incentives, that aims to enhance or preserve the employee's mental or physical health.* With this definition in mind, cardiovascular fitness, nutrition and weight management, measured health indicators like blood lipid levels, mental health and stress management, and chemical dependency treatment all can be considered under the umbrella of comprehensive wellness. Following from the same definition, ergonomics, injury prevention programs, and even educational campaigns to promote driving safety and seatbelt usage can (and should) be viewed as important aspects of wellness.

Much like predictive injury testing, strategies to enhance health and fitness within other wellness dimensions should target *modifiable risk factors*. For instance, "heart" programs incorporate blood lipid level screening, and medical professionals recommend various interventions when certain measurements fall outside normal health parameters. Incidentally, one study estimates the cost of an in-service heart attack for a police officer to be between $400,000 and $750,000 (Bullock, n.d.). *Every* dimension of any wellness program should be approached scientifically with an understanding that mitigating as many risk factors as possible related to an officer's health and wellness has an additive effect which reduces the overall risk of injury, illness, or even death.

Proving the efficacy of wellness programming shouldn't be difficult. There are countless studies supporting the proposition that wellness programs pay for themselves in the long run. For example, Portland Fire Department's 10-year wellness program, designed to teach firefighters better eating and exercise habits, has reduced work-related health expenses by $1500 per firefighter annually (Ceniceros 2011). And, a study of 734 police officers linked sedentary police officers to statistically significant elevated rates of absenteeism and workers' compensation costs, compared to their active counterparts (Greenhow et al. 1991).

The scientific approach should not be limited to identifying and targeting modifiable risk factors. Science and research can help during wellness program implementation as well, especially within the context of motivation and human behavior. Self-determination theory (SDT) distinguishes between behavior motivated by an inherent desire in the behavior itself, divorced of any external pressure to perform (*autonomous motivation*), versus behavior motivated by the presence of deadlines, incentives, or punishment (*controlling motivation*). Researchers have found individuals are more likely to sustain behaviors associated with autonomous motivation and experience a greater degree of satisfaction and enjoyment (Hagger and Chatzisarantis 2012).

Branding, Technology, and Program Organization Are Important Too

Branding may be useful to create sustainable programs. Brands create identity, transcend cultures, and elicit emotion. For all those reasons, wellness and fitness programs should be branded too. The Chicago Police Department, for example, calls their program POWER (Peace Officer Wellness Evaluation Report) (Krainik 2003).

Additionally, technology should be leveraged to promote and support wellness programming and initiatives. There are several companies who host online communities related to various aspects of wellness, enabling clients to create profiles or memberships, design customized fitness programs, and track progress.

It is also recommended that every dimension of wellness

be managed under one umbrella. Mefferd, who has headed Anaheim's wellness program for over a decade, stresses the importance of central control to enable effective branding and to enhance execution of the program. She is assigned to the Training Division.

Next Steps

Agencies wishing to move toward the future of health science should consider the following action steps to integrate predictive injury testing into comprehensive wellness initiatives:

- Analyze your department's workers' compensation data, with a focus on musculoskeletal injuries. Study, tabulate, and organize the injuries by body part, type, and cause. Calculate the cost of these injuries.

- Utilize this data to demonstrate to other stakeholders the need to mitigate work-related injuries. Share studies related to the success of predictive injury testing in mitigating employee injuries. Provide evidence that wellness programs have been proven to be effective in reducing workers' compensation costs.

- Enlist kinesiologists or exercise physiologists who specialize in predictive injury testing to screen your officers. Academy directors should consider the same approach for police recruits.

- Understand predictive injury screening will identify personnel with flawed biomechanics who are most at risk for musculoskeletal injury. Understand the role prescriptive corrective exercise will have in restoring proper movement patterns, while *reducing the likelihood of future injury*. Provide opportunity, incentives, and motivation for your personnel to adopt prescriptive exercise regimens.

- Be sure your predictive injury testing component complements a *comprehensive* wellness initiative. Be sure to also approach other dimensions of your wellness program scientifically, with an emphasis on identifying and targeting modifiable risk factors.

- Share facts, stories, and information with your personnel to demonstrate how a commitment to wellness will enhance their health, fitness, and job satisfaction. Brand the program to promote identity, excitement, and sustainability. Market it using time-tested strategies from private industry. Leverage technology to assist in this area.

- Establish performance goals. Collect comprehensive data related to injuries, predictive injury testing, and other wellness interventions designed to target *modifiable risk factors*. Track progress. Demonstrate your success—*scientifically*.

- Be sure your managers and supervisors set the example and lead the way through a demonstration of their own commitment to health and wellness.

As law enforcement leaders, we have a responsibility for the health and welfare of our workforce. Predictive injury testing offers a proven strategy to promote fitness and increase job satisfaction, while reducing workers' compensation costs and mitigating our officers' risk of future injury.

Conclusion

While predictive injury testing and corrective exercise is not new, it is a relatively unexplored area for law enforcement. Empirical research concerning the efficacy of both public domain screening tests and proprietary screening systems continues to be conducted. What is currently known supports law enforcement administrators exploring how predictive injury testing can be incorporated into broader wellness initiatives designed to target modifiable risk factors that can mitigate injury, reduce health care costs, and enhance job satisfaction. To this end, decision makers should borrow from research and theory related to motivation to develop optimal implementation strategies that promote scientifically-based, sustainable wellness initiatives. During the month that I first participated in the FMS™, I performed corrective exercises daily, and I improved my FMS™ score from 9 to 13. It's a work in progress.

ABOUT CHIEF MIKE HAMEL (RET.)

Chief Mike Hamel is a 29-year law enforcement veteran who recently retired as the Police Chief for the City of Irvine. He was the first police chief to rise through the ranks from police officer to chief from within Irvine PD. Currently, he serves as the Chief Security Operations Officer for Hoag—a healthcare network serving the Orange County community.

Chief Hamel is the Past President of the Orange County Chiefs of Police and Sheriffs Association. He also served as the Governing Board Chair for Waymakers, Inc., a non-profit dedicated to serving the needs of victims, and as a Commissioner for the Orange County Human Relations Commission from 2015 through 2021.

Chief Hamel has been recognized for his work in victim advocacy and creating comprehensive victim services programs. He has received several awards for his work in this area, including the Ambassador of Peace award from the Violence Prevention Coalition of Orange County and the Victim Advocacy Lifetime Achievement Award from Crime Survivors, Inc., and has presented at related conferences nationally.

Chief Hamel holds a Master's degree in Public Policy Administration from California State University, Long Beach; a Master's degree in Applied Computer Science from the University of West Georgia; and a Bachelor of Arts degree in Social Ecology, with an emphasis in

Criminology, Law and Society from the University of California, Irvine.

He is also a graduate of the Sherman Block Supervisory Leadership Institute, the International Association of Chiefs of Police Leadership in Police Organizations Program, and Peace Officer Standards and Training Command College.

PART TWO

Cultivating Resiliency in Law Enforcement

HEATHER WILLIAMS, PsyD

A critical incident is any situation faced by public safety personnel that causes strong emotional or physiological reactions.

In the life of a law enforcement professional, there are endless traumatic experiences that change the lens through which they perceive the world. Some claim, "I'm not normal because of what this job has exposed me to." I disagree. You are normal, but your normal is different, unique, and based upon your reality. Normal is relative to the job you do. The law enforcement lens allows you to trauma bond with your partners and hold your loved ones closer. We in law enforcement know that life and death can happen in an instant. As a result of this truth, we can feel vulnerable and exposed; question our own mortality; and get triggered by the events we have responded to and survived through.

Has anyone ever asked you, "How can you do that job?" I wonder what you answered … because not anyone can or will develop your mindset and expertise in responding to the most horrific situations. You've gone to school, survived the academy, had formal training, maybe military experience, and you've learned on the job. But did you ever take (or have offered to you) a class on learning how to manage the unique stressors and traumas that are unavoidable in this field? The stigma attached to admitting a case or situation rocked you likely keeps you insisting that you're "fine." But are you?

This job "took his soul," says the wife of a retired detective suffering with a post-traumatic stress injury (PTSI). Depression, anxiety, post-traumatic stress disorder (PTSD), alcoholism, infidelity, divorce, and suicide plague law enforcement personnel. Why do some of the bravest men and women who sign up to serve and protect silently suffer from the trauma of the job?

Post-traumatic stress is not just a consequence of seeing war; it is a *psychological injury* that also can impact law enforcement personnel. However, in the last few years, law enforcement has begun to address the consequences of trauma head-on with peer support programs and mental health professionals. Regardless, the stigma and the wall of resistance is still very ingrained in the culture.

The Ripple Effect of Trauma

Think about a rock being thrown into a pond. It creates a number of ripples. Now imagine each ripple as a different group of people connected and impacted by a tragedy. Victims are in the middle, then their family, then witnesses, and then community. But what about the outermost ripples? Who pays attention to and supports those working in and around law enforcement—those people who answer the emergency phone call to 9-1-1; those who respond to the scene to render aid and create safety; those who process the scene and the deceased; and those who work in the aftermath to bring justice to victims of crime? These are our forgotten, and sometimes invisible, law enforcement warriors.

Who asks a dispatcher, a forensic scientist, a crime scene investigator, or a coroner investigator how they are doing after a gruesome crime has been committed? What about the victim advocate who works with the victim's family after a tragedy? Who do they talk to? Who gives them permission to be human in the aftermath of tragedy?

Even the most resilient warriors working in law enforcement have moments when they feel helpless, angry, sad, lonely, and broken. For decades, the culture of law enforcement implied that if you are strong, you do not hurt. If you hurt, you must be weak; and if you are weak, you can't be a good partner on duty or off. Perceived weakness even prohibited promotion. It is time to challenge that belief system. Out of respect for the men and women who serve and protect our communities, it is time to break down that stigma by creating a paradigm shift—one that says that it is an act of strength to be able to talk about what bothers you.

Strength comes in different formats. Strength is growth that can occur after trauma. Strength can be vulnerability and tears. Strength is when you keep working toward healing even when it's emotionally painful. Strength is saying, "I'm sorry and I will learn to do things better for the good of everyone around me." Strength is choosing not to live a numb life, avoiding pain, and hurting those around you. There is no doubt that this job changes you, but it doesn't have to define who you are. You can choose not to give up your core self and let the job take your soul. You have a right to choose to take back control and live the happiest life possible. You have the right to resiliency.

What Is Resiliency?

There are several concepts of resiliency. A common theme is the process of adapting and bouncing back in the face of danger, adversity, and trauma (Southwick et al. 2015). Others include seeking out and using resources; healthy functioning; increased ability to manage physiological reactions; and moving forward post trauma in a positive manner. Note, however, that resiliency is not a simple concept; people may be resilient in one part or phase of their life, but not in another (Southwick et al. 2015).

It's also important to note that not everyone who is, by definition, a first responder will be impacted the same way by an incident. There is significant variation in terms of response to trauma and resiliency. Risk factors for PTSD in law enforcement include a biological or genetic predisposition (Miller 1999). Some people have an innate heightened physiological reaction to traumatic stimuli. Having multiple exposures to traumatic events, along with the occurrence of long-term stressors in life, can accumulate and become a risk for the development of PTSD. Psychological factors such as poor coping and problem solving along with learned helplessness and poor relationships are factors in the risk of developing PTSD (Miller 1999). Lastly, environmental factors like lack of departmental response and support, including social support, can increase risk of maladaptive functioning following a critical incident (Miller 1999).

Genetic, neurobiological, and psychosocial factors all impact an individual's resiliency and response to stress. Regarding genetics, "There is evidence that there are genetic differences in reactivity of the hypothalamic-pituitary-adrenal axis, sympathetic nervous system and serotonergic systems that have been connected to post-traumatic pathology and resilience" (Southwick et al. 2015, p. 2). Neurobiological factors focus on the neural circuits and parts of the brain involved in processing "fear, reward, learning, social connection and emotional regulation" (Southwick et al. 2015, p. 2).

There are a number of psychosocial factors supported by research that have been associated with resiliency. These include optimism; good problem solving, communication, and coping skills; courage; altruism; physical activity; self-mastery or an internal locus of control; ability to have a strategy and anticipate consequences; being sociable;

emotional regulation; emotional intelligence; ability to strategize and anticipate consequences; connection to spirituality or religion; access to social support; a close connection/relationship with someone who feels caring; and a sense of commitment to a goal or mission that is meaningful. Studies have shown that believing in, or honoring, a moral code can facilitate resiliency and that altruism helps build resiliency by focusing attention on others instead of self. Even responding to a traumatic event can help first responders reframe their experience and enhance their feelings of self-confidence while accepting the situation and learning to let go of control they do not have. Physical activity helps increase the ability to focus and make decisions while also enhancing and stabilizing emotional reactions (Southwick et al. 2015). It also suppresses cortisol and increases the production of neurotropic factors which promote the healing and growth of neurons.

Specific to law enforcement, Paton and colleagues (2000) have identified resiliency factors that enable officers to withstand extreme traumatic experiences. These include first-rate training and skill development, an attitude of being a lifelong learner, higher levels of intelligence and problem solving, good verbal and interpersonal communication skills, acceptable emotional control and adaptive coping mechanisms, seeing the positive in situations, and the ability to seek help and support when necessary.

Resiliency is not just a theoretical topic to be taken

lightly. Recognizing the impact of police trauma and its contribution to stress-related disorders, substance abuse, depression, and law enforcement suicide are imperative to helping increase physical and mental health, as well as optimum job functioning in law enforcement personnel (Miller 1999).

It's clear that resiliency is a protective factor in mitigating the effects of a critical incident in first responders (Miller 1999; Paton 2006; Paton and Burke 2007; Evans et al. 2013; Andersen et al. 2015). So, how do individuals and law enforcement organizations collectively build resiliency among officers? Organizations themselves have two roles to play: encouraging social support—both formal and informal—and integrating resiliency training. Furthermore, law enforcement personnel can practice individual psychological tactics and coping strategies to bolster their personal resiliency.

The Role of Social Support in Building Resiliency

Social support, particularly organizational support, greatly influences resiliency in law enforcement professionals. Social support is an umbrella term that encompasses organizational support, peer support, and family support (Miller 1999; Paton 2006; Paton and Burke 2007; Evans et al. 2013; Andersen et al. 2015). Included in defining social support is feeling safe in sharing thoughts and feelings and being able to find meaning in the aftermath of a traumatic event. The ability to find meaning reduces feelings of vulnerability and can help personnel accept the situation for what it was and experience post-traumatic growth (Paton 2006; Paton and Burke 2007; Miller 1999). The term post-traumatic growth was developed by psychologists Richard Tedeschi and Lawrence Calhoun in the mid-1990s. "They teach that people who endure psychological struggle following adversity can often see positive growth afterward" (Collier 2016).

The organizational culture has a direct correlation to law enforcement personnel's level of job satisfaction which relates back to their perception of support by the organization. Support from the senior officers, sergeants, and command staff in law enforcement agencies plays a very important role in personnel's response and recovery in the aftermath of a critical incident. Through their style of communication, a showing of genuine care and concern, and decisions to decrease the stigma of talking about the aftermath of critical incidents, they contribute to increased levels of morale among the troops, team cohesiveness, and a feeling of appreciation (Paton and Burke 2007).

In fact, many law enforcement leaders see the importance of taking care of their troops and making the debrief mandatory. By making attendance mandatory, but participation voluntary, leaders are reducing the stigma and the code of silence that is part of the law enforcement culture (Papazoglou and Andersen 2014). In my experience responding to critical incidents and facilitating critical incident debriefs, command staff who actively respond to a critical incident in the field to support their personnel, and then continue that show of support by attending and participating in the critical incident debrief, are leading by example and creating a cultural shift that shows their personnel that they care.

Better work relationships empower law enforcement professionals to find meaning in their work before a critical incident; thus, they can better adapt in the aftermath of a trauma. Feeling validated and supported by supervisors after the chaos and unpredictability of a critical incident helps first responders manage their perceived lack of control (Paton and Burke 2007). On the other hand, poor organizational response to a critical incident causes many officers to feel more traumatized. They've described feeling "isolation, unsupported, and disempowered" (Papazoglou 2012, p. 205).

Papazoglou suggests that the police organization is responsible for developing the necessary interventions that provide officers with tools for coping and programs that help their personnel develop resiliency. The organization could require a "mental health check-in"—periodic counseling—for all officers (BadgeofLife.com). Or, officers involved in certain types of critical incidents, like an officer involved shooting (OIS), can check in with a mental health professional contracted with the department or someone of their choosing. Additionally, peer support programs have been shown effective in helping personnel get the support they need with professional and personal life stressors and in the aftermath of a critical incident (Papazoglou 2012).

Peer support can be formal, like an agency peer support program, or informal through peer relationships with beat partners, friends in the department, and other colleagues (Techmanski 2014). One of the many reasons peer support teams in law enforcement agencies have been successful is because a peer understands the culture, language, and needs of their brothers and sisters in law enforcement. In their own way, helping the impacted person means offering them the safety to say anything without judgment and allowing them to use language (including profanity) or terms (like police codes, acronyms, etc.) that they might not be comfortable using in front of a non-law enforcement person. Trust and comfort in knowing they will not be judged are keys to receiving effective peer support. In a culture that has a hard time receiving support, peers who provide one-on-one conversation and/or help the impacted party see a mental health professional are both increasing psychological resiliency and changing the departmental culture (Hesketh 2014; Karaffa and Thrasher 2016; Nicoletti et al. 2016).

Evans et al. (2013), in "Police officers' experiences of supportive and unsupportive social interactions following traumatic incidents," discuss social support as one factor that may contribute to well-being and resiliency in first responders. This study explores the nature of social support interactions from the perspective of 19 police officers in in the UK, in different positions and ranks, who had experienced a critical incident but had not developed PTSD. The goal was to understand the types of support that may promote resiliency.

Results suggested a number of themes. Whether to talk about incidents or not was a central theme. Talking about reactions to a traumatic event was seen as risky because of the culture of police work in the UK. Participants explained that they feared being perceived as weak by their peers. Yet, despite these perceptions, participants strongly endorsed the idea that talking about an incident was helpful. Talking was seen as imperative for maintaining relationships at work and in their personal relationships at home. By talking to peers, the officers realized they were not alone; that, in turn, reduced feelings of shame or second guessing and became an outlet for processing the traumatic event (Evans et al. 2013).

While having an option to talk was valued, officers needed to feel in control of when and where they would talk. Participants had mixed opinions on whether formal opportunities to talk, like group debriefing and individual counseling, should be optional or mandatory. Mandatory critical incident debriefings reduced the stigma of talking about an incident. Supervisor support also influenced the decision to talk about an incident. A supervisor who was perceived as supportive was the greatest factor to enhance officer well-being, thereby increasing resiliency in the aftermath of a critical incident (Evans et al. 2013).

Supportive interactions with peers who used "selfless listening," or who listened without judgment; who were empathetic; and who validated officers' reactions were identified across the study as helpful in both formal and informal relationships (Evans et al. 2013, p. 5). Feeling as though they could talk if needed appears to be a crucial finding in officers' feelings of support (Evans et al. 2013). The buy-in and support from the leadership in developing and sustaining peer support programs while respecting and upholding confidentiality policies can be the impetus for creating a cultural shift that gives law enforcement personnel the trust to talk about the impact of a critical incident. Many first responders preferred to talk to peers, versus family and non-law enforcement friends, about work-related reactions, tactics, and experiences resulting from a critical incident (Miller 1999; Evans et al. 2013; Papazoglou and Andersen 2014; Andersen et al. 2015). This was their way of protecting their loved ones from what they saw and experienced (Evans et al. 2013; Miller 1999). As a psychologist specializing in treating public safety personnel, I encourage law enforcement professionals to ask their loved ones, "How much do you want to hear?" rather than protect or assume they can't handle it. This is important to prevent disconnection and isolation and increase support at home.

An important finding is the concept of humor and banter as a means of support and increased resiliency. Humor can help both from a psychological and physiological perspective. Humor creates emotional distance from the incident, reduces adrenaline, increases dopamine, brings perspective and meaning, and can increase the adaptive capacity of a first responder (Brooks et al. 2016). The use of humor and banter in the aftermath of a critical incident were central features of interactions with partners and supervisors. Humor appeared to play a positive role in dealing with uncomfortable emotions, which helped participants reframe the event and create meaning. Humor also created social bonds that contributed to a feeling of group cohesiveness and safety, which helps in the mitigation of emotional reactions resulting from the traumatic event. The overall perception of support increases development of resiliency in law enforcement professionals.

In sum, leadership contributes to creating a positive organizational climate by creating safety in sharing thoughts and feelings connected to a critical incident by partnering with their peer support program, creating policy that mandates check-ins with mental health professionals given certain types of critical incidents, encouraging the attendance of the critical incident debriefing and, when appropriate, participating in that debriefing (Evans et al. 2013; Chae and Boyle 2013; Shakespeare-Finch et al. 2015; Paton 2006).

Yuan et al. (2011) found that law enforcement professionals who experienced an increased level of self-worth, had good social support, good social adjustment, and saw the world through a positive lens experienced lowered post-traumatic stress symptoms following a critical incident.

The Role of Law Enforcement Resiliency Training

Resiliency training—or developing "psychological armor" (Miller 1999)—helps law enforcement personnel build resiliency. Training includes stress inoculation training, hardiness training, pre-crisis psychoeducation, and cognitive-behavioral techniques to decrease the physiological response to stress such as mindfulness and progressive relaxation.

From the beginning, law enforcement training should incorporate building the resiliency of recruits, so that when they graduate and become officers, they have developed psychological and tactical armor that makes them able to adjust and adapt to fluid situations and maintain their mental toughness (Miller 2014). Resiliency training increases feelings of competence and mastery in decision making and tactics, and enhances law enforcement officers' perception of control. Resiliency training builds confidence and feelings of self-efficacy; those, in turn, increase the development of resiliency and contribute to improved health and positive outcomes post critical incident (Arnetz et al. 2013; Arnetz et al. 2009; Backman et al. 1997).

Police work is stressful and can cause several mental health issues. From the beginning, in pre-academy and at the academy, recruits are taught to be strong and stoic. Historically, the culture of law enforcement perceives asking for help as weakness. In fact, a study of 178 male police officers found that they avoided seeing a mental health professional because of the stigma attached in going to a "shrink" for help (Papazoglou and Andersen 2014). Thus, trauma often isolates people in the police culture because of this stigma. One way to address this barrier and create a cultural shift to promote resiliency in police officers is through training at the beginning of their career while in the academy.

According to Papazoglou, missing from police training programs is education on the impact of trauma for officers who are exposed to high levels of stress and trauma; the normalization of asking for help; and the purpose and benefits of peer support programs. To build trust and partnership with recruits, a police academy should utilize a student-centered training environment (Papazoglou and Andersen 2014). This environment can enhance a student's adaptive coping skills, physical fitness, and effectiveness. Student-centered training could increase a sense of connection between recruit and police trainer that can model creating close relationships. These close relationships serve as an integral component for creating a sense of belonging, promoting resiliency, and reducing isolation in the aftermath of a critical incident (Papazoglou and Andersen 2014).

Research and practice-based recommendations include having police trainers come from law enforcement agencies and be a part of the police culture. This enhances their credibility and gets buy-in from the recruits from the beginning. Police trainers have a unique opportunity to influence the health and longevity of the recruits' careers in law enforcement by establishing an acceptance of talking about police stress and trauma. It's also recommended to include the following topics in the training curriculum: psychoeducation on the mental and physical impact of traumatic events; reducing stigma in the police culture by helping recruits understand emotions like fear, anxiety, and terror experienced during the course of a career in law enforcement are normal and not signs of weakness; and education on the value of peer support and other programs that can assist with mental health concerns (Papazoglou and Andersen 2014).

Some comprehensive programs to increase resiliency already have been designed. By learning to control perceptions, feelings, thoughts, and reactions through progressive rehearsal or stress inoculation training before a critical incident occurs, officers develop a core of resiliency that is both mental and operational (Miller 1999).

Stress inoculation training focuses on the person's beliefs in their ability to cope with the stressors. The training involves three phases. The first phase is educational. The second phase is increasing a skill set or rehearsing what was just learned in a classroom setting. The third phase includes a practice phase where participants practice using the coping skills learned during phase two (Southwick et al. 2015). This type of training is used in law enforcement settings so that officers can learn tactics and condition themselves to respond to high stress situations. In the aftermath of an officer involved shooting, it is not uncommon to hear the officer say, "My training kicked in and I did what I was supposed to do."

Simulation exercises also help stress inoculate officers in responding to high stress incidents. Trainings that explain realistic outcomes and build positive beliefs promote an ability to distinguish personal and situational constraints, which gives officers an opportunity to learn and increase future mastery of, and confidence in, their tactics, decision making, and responses to critical incidents. Another program to build resiliency is hardiness training. Hardiness is a psychological concept that is made up of three interrelated components, which include commitment, control, and challenge. Commitment refers to the ability to turn a tragedy into something meaningful. The second component, control, regards feelings of control or believing that one has influence over life events. This way of thinking prevents long-term feelings of helplessness. Challenge, the third component, is the capacity to experience stressful and adverse events as challenges rather than threats, while also seeing the situation as an opportunity for growth. There is evidence that hardiness can be learned and increased through training that teaches people how to address feelings of perceived loss of control, cope with stress, and build on the ability to give and receive social support (Southwick et al. 2015).

Psychoeducation training is yet another resiliency-building technique. Psychoeducation helps to front-load the process with first responders by creating awareness. With this awareness police officers learn that the acute stress reactions or post-traumatic symptoms experienced in the aftermath of a tragedy are normal. Normalizing reactions through education and real-world examples helps to validate that they are not alone, aren't weak, and aren't going crazy. I've experienced this firsthand. It's very common during my *"Impact of Trauma for Law*

Enforcement" class for students to approach during the breaks to discuss or disclose their reactions to a critical incident. It's not uncommon to have a student say, "I wished I had known this 20 years ago when I started my career."

For psychoeducation to be useful in resiliency training, there is imperative to choose the right instructors. Educators who are police personnel bring credibility and increase the likelihood of a cultural shift that gives permission to law enforcement personnel to be human in response to critical incidents and that "It's ok to not be ok." This empowers personnel to understand that what they are experiencing isn't mental weakness and that talking about what they experienced can help reduce post-traumatic stress symptoms and increase post-traumatic growth (Papazoglou and Andersen 2014).

Overall, researchers found that psychoeducation led to improvement in health measures before, during, and after a critical incident. It also increases "positive emotion, vitality, reduced negative emotion and depressive symptoms, and improved self-regulation in response to stress" (Andersen et al. 2015, p. 5).

New types of resiliency training that are currently underutilized are cognitive-behavioral techniques that manage stress reactions. Training that is psychological in nature or perceived as "touchy feely" will take time to integrate into law enforcement training and culture in general. Yet their use is growing.

Mindfulness training is one cognitive-behavioral technique of resiliency building that is new to police work. Lt. Richard Goerling with the U.S. Coast Guard is at the head of a movement that provides a different type of support for officers—one that perceives mindfulness as a protective factor for them personally and for the communities they serve. "We as a profession cannot be tactically sound, operationally savvy, guard people, and put our life on the line for people we may not ever meet if we can't see or handle the tragedy and heartache that's part of our every day job" (Goerling 2016). Empirical research and science show that mindfulness is helpful. Moreover, the scientific evidence encourages officers to find legitimacy in the concept, which means more openness to trying it (Goerling 2016).

In "Officer Safety Corner: The Role of Mindfulness Training in Policing a Democratic Society," Lt. Goerling addresses the reality of the police culture and how it often takes a large-scale critical incident like a line of duty death or suicide for a department to create a wellness program that addresses the psychological impact of police work. Historically, these programs were reactive and left to the individual officer to manage. But, he argues, reactive models of wellness are not going to prevent complex and long-term police trauma. Rather, a preventative holistic model that includes mindfulness and addresses the mental, physical, and spiritual wellness of personnel will build resiliency (Goerling 2016). According to Richard Strozzi-Heckler, who has trained U.S. Army Special Forces in meditation and mindfulness,

"Teaching meditation to police officers makes sense, culturally and scientifically. Meditation speaks to the warrior soul and teaches critical skills in self-awareness" (Goerling 2016, p. 2).

Police training programs spend a lot of money and energy on situational awareness, operations, and tactics. Mindfulness training has been shown to improve neuroplasticity of the brain which results in developing pathways to increased operational, mental, and psychological resiliency (Goerling 2016). Police organizations that proactively integrate mindfulness training into their culture from the leadership down are building the adaptive capacity of their personnel. First responders who develop a warrior mindset that includes mindfulness learn to respond to a critical incident, work through the process of adapting in the aftermath, and can become mentally stronger than where they started—all of which can lead to post-traumatic growth (Goerling 2016).

Other cognitive-behavioral techniques use relaxation practices like progressive muscle relaxation, deep breathing, and guided imagery. Mind-body connection to resiliency training can include yoga, dance therapy, and tai chi. Journaling is another self-directed, non-stigmatizing coping strategy that can help law enforcement personnel. Exploring irrational beliefs and reducing over general-izations that cause negative thought patterns also reduce depression and cynicism in law enforcement professionals. Humor is often used as a coping strategy; it creates bonds and helps with healing after a traumatic event. Lastly, police trainers can model trusting relationships and active listening to increase a recruit's self-control and efficacy. New police officers who feel a sense of control may be better able to cope with organizational and operational stress while remaining resilient in the face of personal adversity or a traumatic event (Papazoglou and Andersen 2014).

The various trainings for resiliency—stress inoculation, hardiness, pre-crisis psychoeducation, and cognitive-behavioral techniques—have a number of benefits to personnel including increased self-awareness and competence, reduction in stress responses during a crisis, and self-mastery. Through proactive resiliency training, organizations create a culture that increases the mental, physical, and spiritual health of personnel, which, in effect, increases resiliency in the law enforcement warriors who serve and protect the community.

Your Individual Role in Building Resiliency

You recharge your cell phones as the battery is depleted throughout the day. Why aren't you investing time each day to "recharge" *your* battery? There is a myriad of psychological and coping strategies that have proven helpful to mitigate burnout, compassion fatigue, post-traumatic stress, and other mental health issues. Here are some ideas that may help you.

1. **Transitioning from work to home.** What do you need to transition from being "on" and in a sympathetic state of stress to relaxing at home? Do you need to "shower off the day?" Do you need to watch TV or sports, play a video game, talk to your loved one, workout, play with your child or pet, dig in the garden, or cook? Whatever your mode of transition, create a plan and communicate it to your loved ones at home to increase their support and mitigate conflict from lack of communication.

2. **Hobbies/interests.** Do you have a hobby? Is there something you "usta" do that you don't do anymore because life responsibilities took over? Is there some thing you've always wanted to do, but convinced yourself it wasn't that important or you don't have time? One way to jump-start a hobby is to schedule it on a calendar. Set a time frame; give yourself permission for self-care the same as you would if you had a doctor's appointment or you were going to your child's sporting event.

3. **Faith/religion/spirituality.** This is an aspect of life that is private and personal. What do you believe? Would you find value in participating in religious services? Is there value in reading religious texts or participating in a study or group at your institution?

4. **Emotional awareness.** "Feeling" is the "F word" of law enforcement. However, consider exploring whether you really recognize or understand your

reactions and triggers. Can you communicate to those people in your lives what you are thinking, feeling, and needing? Can you explain your behavior to yourself? Others? If you find this a challenge, contact your contracted mental health professional or read articles and books or watch YouTube videos on emotional intelligence.

5. **Communication.** This is incredibly important for overall emotional wellness, but communication specifically aids in building healthy relationships at work and at home. How do you communicate your needs? Starting with "I" is the best way to communicate to others. "I am hurt by the comment you made." "I feel disrespected when you ignore my input." When you start with "I," you take responsibility for your thoughts, feelings, and reactions. Nobody can say, "No you don't." When you communicate and start with "You," you are placing blame on the other person; their natural reaction is to become defensive and either make excuses, deflect, or defend. This creates an interaction and conflict that can feel impossible to resolve.

6. **Exercise.** There is a lot of research that explains why exercise is good for reducing stress, anxiety, burnout, insomnia, and other symptoms of trauma. When you exercise, you produce endorphins, dopamine, norepinephrine, and serotonin—all of which help you feel good while reducing the stress hormones cortisol and adrenaline.

7. **Food as fuel.** Nutrition is fuel for your body and your mind. The choices you make can affect your mood, level of anxiety, energy, focus, and perceived sense of control (in a world where we often feel out of control). For more suggestions on making healthy food choices, see the first three chapters in Part Three.

8. **Sleep.** Law enforcement officers struggle with sleep-related disorders as a result of shift work, stress, high caseloads, conflict at home, and organizational stress. Sleep experts recommend creating a sleep routine. This routine can include, but is not limited to, the following activities.

- Shower or bathe before bedtime—warm water relaxes the body and mind.

- Stretch or practice yoga before bedtime. These activities counteract the build-up of lactic acid in your muscles from exercise and from the weight of equipment and stress you carry on your body. They help relax the body and the mind.

- Using white or pink noise, like static, fan blowing, waves crashing, rain, or thunderstorms, can shift your mind away from any thoughts that are occupying it and preventing sleep. White and pink noise tells the brain waves to slow down, which then prepares you for more restful, deep sleep. Deep sleep is restorative and REM sleep is important for processing your day and the production of serotonin. Serotonin is a neurotransmitter and our "policing center." Optimal levels of serotonin increases our cognitive ability to make logical versus emotional decisions, decreases insomnia, and decreases levels of depression and anxiety. Sleep is imperative to your well-being and level of functioning at work and at home.

- Utilize the 20-minute rule. Sleep experts recommend that if you toss and turn for 20 minutes, get up, read something lighthearted, watch a funny video, or have a snack that is nutritious, not sugary or fatty.

- Write it down/get it out. If you ruminate about to-do lists, what your boss said to you, or the conflict with your significant other, get a journal or type your thoughts in your phone. Make a to-do list and email it to yourself.

- Set boundaries with media/social media before bedtime. We've all watched or read something that upsets us and prevents us from going to sleep. I encourage you to give your brain at least 30 minutes to relax without added "noise" of the news or social media.

- Practice combat breathing (also known as box breathing). Inhale through the nose for four seconds, hold for four seconds, then exhale through the mouth for four seconds or longer. This breathing technique tells the nervous system that it's ok to calm down.

- Try supplements for sleep like melatonin, magnesium, ashwagandha, or 5-HTP. If you are on prescription medication, please consult with your medical doctor before starting any supplements.

9. **Meditation.** Meditation teaches law enforcement officers how to be present in the moment. Research shows that meditation reduces stress, anxiety, and is a preventative measure that equips police personnel to perform through occupational trauma with greater capacity for awareness. It helps calm the nervous system, increases cognitive performance, and makes you more compassionate, empathetic, and nonjudgmental.

10. **Humor.** Using humor reduces cortisol and adrenaline while it increases dopamine, serotonin, and endorphins. It provides a safe way to distance self and share emotions; reduces stress, anxiety, depression, and loneliness; creates feelings of control; and reduces interpersonal tension. Quick-witted, gallows humor is necessary for longevity in law enforcement.

11. **Pets.** Many people consider their pets as "emotional comfort animals" even without the certification because of the positive attributes that pets bring to their lives. Pets create social connection and bonding; they love unconditionally;

they aid in relaxation; and they improve overall mental, social, and physiological health.

12. **Therapy with a Mental Health Professional.** I encourage all law enforcement professionals to have a relationship with a culturally competent mental health professional. Being able to check in when there is a situation at home, work, or after responding to a critical incident is important.

13. **Annual Wellness Check-in.** More law enforcement departments are looking at how to integrate mental health as part of their "wellness programs." Rather than making annual wellness check-ins mandatory, it may be best to incentivize participation. I believe that the annual wellness check-in is not therapy, but, rather, a semi-structured appointment to assess all aspects of wellness including, but not limited to: informal stress and sleep assessments; discussion on physical health, burnout, compassion fatigue, critical incident stress, relationship health, and organizational stress; and assessment of resources and referrals.

14. **Get organized.** Working in law enforcement often means reacting to someone's worst day. Ultimately, this can lead to feeling that you are not in control, which means you will try to either control others or find ways to feel in control. Getting organized can help you feel back in control.

Conclusion

In the aftermath of personal adversity, work related stress, or trauma, you have an opportunity to use your experiences in ways that help you grow. The journey to post-traumatic growth can be painful because it can take a lot of time, mental and emotional energy, and struggle.

There is no doubt that you have been on your own journey. I'd like to challenge you to take a more in-depth look at your journey and decide to pay it forward. What exactly does this mean? For each of you, this will look different, but it can mean helping change the culture of your department by validating and normalizing your partners' and peers' thoughts, feelings, and reactions to the stressors and traumas of job. It can also mean attending a critical incident debrief, sharing your reactions after a critical incident to allow others to feel safe doing the same, or joining the peer support team. Each small step you take to "pay it forward" helps build a culture of support, and support is a powerful key to building more resilient law enforcement personnel.

ABOUT HEATHER WILLIAMS, PsyD

Dr. Heather Williams has worked in and around law enforcement for the last 22 years. She worked in Probation, Victim Services, and started a Crisis Response Team after recognizing that critical incidents create a ripple of impact. In 2014, after developing the Orange County Sheriff's Department Peer Support Program, Dr. Williams was hired as their first Regional Peer Support Coordinator. She coordinated a team of almost 100 OCSD personnel, responded to critical incidents, provided training, and coordinated an emotional wellness campaign. Dr. Williams also co-founded the Orange County Association of Peer Supporters (OCAPS).

After spending five years as the Regional Peer Support Coordinator, Dr. Williams elected to take her passion to another level and, in 2019, established *Premier First Responder Psychological Services*. As a licensed psychologist, she provides culturally competent services to individuals and couples and assists public safety professionals with treatment in Eye Movement Desensitization and Reprocessing (EMDR). Additionally, Dr. Williams helps public safety departments develop and sustain peer support programs, provides 24/7 critical incident response, facilitates a two-step model of critical incident debriefing, and provides active shooter response and recovery response services.

Dr. Williams offers training on several topics including, but not limited to: Wellness & Resiliency in Public Safety, POST (Peace Officer Standards & Training) Certified Peer

Support Training, and Critical Incident Response for Peer Support. She speaks at conferences and to academies about the stressors and traumas of public safety with the goal of creating a culture of wellness and building resiliency.

Dr. Williams has an MA in Criminal Justice and a PsyD in Psychology. She is also a POST certified instructor. Dr. Williams is a member of the Psychological Services Section with the International Association of Chiefs of Police, the Director of Mental Health Services for Halos4Heroes (a nonprofit serving first responders), and Vice President/Director of Peer Support & Mental Health for the National Law Enforcement Cancer Support Foundation.

PART THREE

Thriving in Law Enforcement

OFFICER JOHN D. DARBY (RET.)

In April 2008, my partner and I responded to a shots fired call at a large cemetery. After we gathered information from the witness, we entered the cemetery grounds to investigate. As we approached the area where the suspect had been last seen, he ambushed us with a shotgun blast at close range from a concealed position near the roadway. Miraculously, the gunfire missed our patrol vehicle, and we were able to evacuate the scene and contain the suspect to the area. A short while later, other officers and I had a second officer involved shooting (OIS) with the suspect, and he was taken into custody.

During the incident, I sustained severe acoustic trauma to my ear. After months of excruciating pain, nausea, and dizziness, I was told by my medical team that I would have to leave law enforcement, as my ear and vestibular system could no longer tolerate the loud noise of the job.

With my career over, depression quickly set in. I knew I

was in a vicious cycle of pain and stress, and I needed to do something—anything—to recover my health and well-being. I began researching methods to manage chronic pain and restore inner balance. Western medicine offered little to alleviate my condition, so I sought and discovered answers to my challenges in Eastern medicine, which addresses the whole person—body, mind, and spirit.

Although I write from the perspective of a retiree, the strategies that follow are ideal for anyone in law enforcement. I will briefly discuss meditation, empowering the mind, physical fitness, and a simple eating plan that worked for me. No matter your circumstances, I hope some of these ideas that I find useful can benefit you too.

Morning Meditation

In the morning, immediately after waking, I allow for a few moments of unstructured meditation to prepare me for the day ahead. This practice of simply watching my thoughts until they gradually subside allows for greater control of my mind, and, as a result, I am more lucid and calmer throughout the day. For me, meditation is not so much a "practice" as it is a feeling of "relaxing" into what some teachers call the "natural state." When meditation became a habit, I experienced a simple but powerful realization: *I am not my thoughts.* I watch thoughts and give them attention; yet, I always have the freedom to discard them if they affect my inner calm. Over time, a profound silence emerged from within, and now I can carry it throughout most of the day, even in the midst of activity. I am not rigid with the time I allot for meditation in my morning sessions—usually 15–45 minutes does the trick for me. Rupert Spira, a meditation teacher with a large following on YouTube, has a unique approach to investigating the mind that has proven quite helpful to me.

If sitting still is not your thing, there are several other meditation methods available to you. One I find beneficial is a *moving meditation* known as "qigong" (pronounced: "chi-kung"). Qigong is an ancient method for synchronizing the breath, mind, and body with gentle movements that are simple to learn but have a profound effect on the body. It has been practiced in Asia for over 4000 years. The qigong "set" can be done in just a few minutes a day. I studied qigong in the attempt to lessen my ear and neck pain; surprisingly, it was the only modality that worked. There are several styles of qigong (I learned three), but I find the most benefit in a simple qigong form known as "the Basic Eight," taught by Grand Master Hong Liu, at qimaster.com.

Morning Affirmations

I (re)discovered affirmations recently; they are extraordinarily effective in setting a positive tone for the day. In the post-pandemic world, many of us awaken to an onslaught of negative news stories that pummels our minds daily.

If I do not "program" my mind with words of my own choosing, the news and social media outlets are happy to do it for me.

With this in mind, I created a series of powerful affirmations that I recite aloud to myself in the morning after meditation. I say them with conviction, sometimes playing uplifting music as I do this. I invite you to create some affirmations of your own that inspire and uplift, and reflect on them throughout your day. I am quite amazed at the results I experience from the consistent application of this fundamental self-help practice. By keeping the affirmations in mind, I easily handle negative situations that arise each day. With recovery or retirement comes the likelihood of more free time, so it is imperative to keep the mind sharp and vigilant. Do not let outside (media) sources dictate how you act, think, and feel. Meditation and affirmations help bring the mind and body under control so that they serve you.

Fitness Through Resistance Training

I began serious weight training during my military service overseas. Thirty years later, my passion for lifting has not waned in the slightest. The benefits of resistance training are legion. Moreover, for me, having the same strength and mobility that I had in my 30s has been of utmost importance. I currently train each body part at least twice a week; one session is moderately heavy in poundage (for strength), and one session is moderate in poundage (for muscle growth/hypertrophy). To enhance recovery and prevent burnout, I take a week off from strength training every couple of months. During this time, I bike, hike, and walk instead.

While many law enforcement officers have had some experience with lifting in their lifetimes, I cannot emphasize enough the importance of educating yourself on proper form and controlled movements; this becomes even more necessary later in life as the potential for injury increases. I can honestly say that intelligent weightlifting with good form and moderate poundage has been the single most important factor in maintaining my health and quality of life during midlife.

Of course, weight training may not be for you, but staying as active as possible for your level of health is most certainly a good idea. My favorite no-impact exercise is brisk walking. I competed in long distance trail running for many years, but in my late 40s, I lost my passion for the sport as the injuries became more frequent and the recovery time was much longer. I replaced running with daily hiking/walking, and I enjoy it just as much. Do not underestimate the health benefits of walking. You can burn hundreds of calories in a brisk 45-minute walk.

With regard to managing calories, I'll share a few words about how I lost 40 pounds of unhealthy body weight in my late 40s and kept it off.

Never Diet Again

Before I share my diet plan, understand that this is what I did to lose weight. After seeing my results, some friends also tried it and had similar success. However, this way of eating may not fit your lifestyle or your health situation, so it's always advisable to consult a physician before you begin.

I worked as a personal trainer in my early 20s and learned about the different approaches to nutrition. In the decades that followed, I was always on the hunt for the perfect way of eating, even trying some of the recent popular diets, like intermittent fasting and the ketogenic diet. And while I initially experienced positive results with both of these approaches, I always found myself going back to my old way of eating and regaining the weight I had lost. After all of my dietary adventures, I discovered that basic calorie counting (with some modifications) was, by far, the most successful and easiest method I have ever encountered.

The crux of my problem was simple. I was overweight, which likely meant I ate more calories than I burned. So, my plan was to create a small caloric deficit each day, and slowly lose the unwanted weight. I wanted to do it gradually as to not shock my body with rapid weight loss and enable my metabolism to slowly adjust to a lower bodyweight. Tracking my calories and "macros" (protein/carbohydrate/fat grams) seemed to be the answer.

The maxim "what gets measured gets managed" is a key

point regarding food intake. We may be proficient at tracking aspects of our financial life, but many of us are oblivious to the calories and nutrients we consume on a daily basis. When I first learned of food tracking and "flexible dieting," I dreaded the idea of buying a digital food scale and counting calories and protein grams. However, some interesting things happened when I started logging my daily food intake. I learned about— and prepared—healthy, filling meals with a lower caloric density that satiated my appetite. For example, I started including a huge bowl of spinach salad with lunch and dinner to mitigate hunger. Raw spinach is a low-calorie, nutrient-dense food that suppresses my hunger. I enjoyed discovering low-calorie food replacements for my old high-calorie staples.

After 30-plus years of eating, I was finally able to manage my caloric intake and get it under control. I would still cheat occasionally with my favorite comfort foods but did my best to be accountable to my food log and stay within my caloric allotment for each day. If I had a bad day or two, I would not beat myself up for it. Life happens, we all do it. When the binge was done, I was back at it with zero guilt, working my plan. Within six months, I had lost nearly 40 pounds, my waist size dropped six inches, and my severe high blood pressure returned to normal.

If this sounds like something you may want to try, below are some tips to get you started.

- Consider working with a personal trainer or nutritionist

who is proficient in macros/flexible dieting. Many dietary professionals have shifted to this way of eating in recent years.

- Research "IIFYM" (If It Fits Your Macros) and flexible dieting. YouTube and Instagram are great sources for information. I like Instagram because the information is direct and to the point. Many health and fitness professionals use these mediums exclusively to reach their audience.

- "Lose It!" and "MyFitnessPal" are smartphone apps for food tracking and determining one's ideal caloric intake based on age, bodyweight, activity level, and weight loss goals. I can log a whole day's food in a minute with these tools. I wish I had these when I first started out.

- Learn how to measure your food accurately. A true tablespoon of peanut butter is about 16 grams. Be wary of a "spoonful" of peanut butter; it can vary greatly in its caloric content depending on the size of the spoon. I like big spoonfuls of peanut butter as much as the next person, but it can sabotage your progress. Use a food scale to ensure accuracy.

- Track your weekly and monthly progress. Get a high-quality scale, annotate your body measurements with a tape measure, and take before and after photos. You will be glad you did.

- Plateaus are inevitable, especially as you near your target weight. Some can last days or weeks. Stay on your plan and be patient.

This concludes my contribution. Thank you for allowing me to share my strategies on how to thrive with you. I wish you good health and happiness on your journey.

ABOUT OFFICER JOHN D. DARBY (RET.)

John D. Darby is a retired police officer with the Glendale Police Department and a USAF Security Police veteran of Operation Desert Shield. He served as a bodyguard for several high-profile clients in Los Angeles, and is a former self-defense/defensive tactics instructor for law enforcement. He holds a brown belt in Kuk Sool Won™ and is an avid practitioner of the energy arts of qigong and tai chi chuan.

He is currently a full-time nomad drifting throughout the southwest USA. He enjoys studying Eastern philosophy, playing guitar, staying fit, and writing.

It's Not Too Late:
Fulfillment in Life and Law Enforcement

CHIEF CHARLES CELANO (RET.)

As I walked out of the cardiologist's office with a stunned look on my face, I still could not believe what I had just heard …

"Mr. Celano, we have some bad news for you. You have coronary artery disease."

It was less than an hour earlier that I walked into that same office with my head held high, not a care in the world, ready to take the CT scan of my heart. "What could possibly happen?" I thought. "There is no heart disease in my family; I exercise regularly; and I even run in 5Ks, 10Ks, and triathlons. My diet is OK, not the worst in the world. This will simply be a run-of-the-mill heart scan and my results will come up roses."

As a 47-year-old male, I was in the 90th percentile for my age and gender, meaning that if you lined up 99 men my age in a room along with me, 89 of them would have a healthier heart than mine. To make things worse, the calcification found on the scan was centralized in the left anterior descending artery (LAD), otherwise known as the "widow maker."

Who came up with that nickname anyway?

I came face to face with my mortality that day, and I was truly at a loss for how to move forward. I had spent the last 27 years of my life as a police officer for a medium-sized city in Orange County, California. I had an amazing career. I worked a variety of assignments, was promoted up through the ranks in the second half of my career, and landed in the Office of the Chief of Police for the last five years. I was truly blessed and then it all came crashing down on me, like a rogue wave out of nowhere.

I went home, told my wife, and we had a long serious talk about our future. What about our five children? What about my grandchildren that I would have someday? Would I even be around to meet them and watch them grow up? What if I left my career at that point, before retirement eligibility age? How would we live? How would we pay the bills? As these thoughts swirled around in my head, my amazing wife offered her support, no matter the decision. I told her I could not just quit. I was not a quitter, and I still had two years left of eligibility before I could truly retire. I decided to just stick it out!

My crucible moment came a few months later when I was tucking my son, Anthony, into bed one night. It was a rare evening where I didn't have a community event, council meeting, or rubber chicken dinner to attend. I relished those times when I was able to tuck my sons into bed. That particular night, as I bent over to give Anthony a hug and kiss goodnight, he suddenly asked me, "Dad, when are you going to retire?" This question jolted me a bit, since I never discuss my retirement plans, work stress, or health-related matters with my kids. As far as they were concerned, Dad was Superman.

"I am not sure buddy … why do you ask?" I replied.

In the most innocent and heartfelt tone, he said, "I just think you would feel better."

My heart felt like it sank into the pit of my stomach. I didn't have to tell him how I felt or show him the heart scan results or share my fear and trepidation with him. He could see it on my face. He could sense it from the way I carried myself. In this brief exchange, Anthony helped me to change the course and direction of my life forever. And in a way, he saved me!

After some heartfelt discussions with my wife, kids, and close friends, I decided it was time to pull the plug on my law enforcement career. A career cut short from the ultimate goal. In triathlon parlance, we call that a "DNF"—Did Not Finish. But I knew one thing: I wasn't going to let the job kill me.

The job of a police officer is amazing in many ways. Where

else can we get such variety and excitement every single day? No two days are the same … no two calls are the same. And the reality is we have the power and ability to make a positive difference in the lives of others every day. It may not seem like it sometimes, but we really do.

But as amazing as this job is, there is a dark side. No one should have to see the things we see. The late nights, long hours, missed birthday parties, canceled vacations all take their toll on cops—physically, emotionally, and spiritually. If we allow it to, this job can and will consume us. It can make us cold, callous, desensitized, and cynical.

Police officers deal with a tremendous amount of stress in our lives, and sometimes we seek out coping mechanisms that are not necessarily in our best interests. Instead of hitting the gym after our shift, we head to the bar; instead of going home and sharing with our spouse the difficult call we handled that day, we seek comfort in someone else, which leads to infidelity; instead of confiding in someone we trust about the pain we feel, we do everything we can to numb that pain. But numbing it doesn't make it go away. It just hides the pain for a while.

These are the dirty little secrets in this profession—alcoholism, divorce, domestic disputes, and substance abuse (particularly painkillers)—we don't talk about them because we don't want to talk about them. It's too painful to talk about them, but we need to start having these courageous conversations with one another.

There is a crisis of culture in law enforcement that stigmatizes and marginalizes police officers who show any signs of emotional struggle. Many of us, when we started the job, were told, "Just suck it up kid … do your job … on to the next call." It wasn't ok to cry; it wasn't ok to show that the last fatal traffic collision you were on had an impact on you because the 16-year-old killed in the crash reminded you of your own child. "Just suck it up … that's part of the job." This culture needs to change.

As a problem solver by nature, I defaulted to that mode as soon as I walked out of the cardiologist's office that day. How would I "solve" this problem? How would I fix this heart disease? What steps could I take to mitigate the damage being done to my heart?

I broke down the problem in a systematic and methodical way, as I have done with many problems I have faced in my life. The first step was to learn as much as I possibly could about coronary artery disease: it's origins, symptoms, causes, and treatments.

From there, I needed to learn as much as I could about the necessary lifestyle changes that would help my cause. I read hundreds of books, articles, white papers, blog posts, etc., in my quest to find the answers to all of my questions. There is an infinite amount of information out there for us—some good and some not so good. The best strategy I found was to keep it simple. The more I simplified things, the more I realized I could actually achieve some level of success moving forward. This journey took me the better part of six months, but as a result, I came up with a plan that would ultimately work for me.

It all boils down to two aspects for me: *systems* and *intentionality*. These two concepts complement and feed one another when it comes to health and wellness. Implementing systems and devoting energy to being as intentional as possible made all the difference in the world; together, they countered my natural tendencies to fall back into the old ways that obviously did not work for me.

I am a huge fan of systems. I construct them in my life around four foundational principles of wellness that I came up with:

1) Intentional Exercise;
2) Intentional Nutrition;
3) Intentional Sleep; and
4) Intentional Mindfulness.

The more systematic I am in my approach, the less likely I will "fall off the wagon" and revert to counter-productive habits. Systems take the form of things like morning routines, journaling, calendaring, task lists, and incentive-based goals. When I put systems in place, they help keep me on track, which takes much of the decision-making out of my hands.

For example, if I have a run scheduled for the following morning (notice I said "scheduled," meaning it is literally on my schedule), I will place my running clothes out in the bathroom and have my water bottle already filled with my hydration mix and ready to go. My work clothes for the day will already be in my gym bag, in my car! Why? Because it makes it a lot harder to back out of the run with all of these pieces in place. Once the alarm goes off at 4:45 a.m., my brain will start talking me out of the run: "You don't have to go this early … it's still dark outside, could be dangerous … you rode your bike last night, you need more rest … wow this bed is nice and warm … you know how important rest is, don't you?" And on and on. I have to immediately fight against these self-limiting thoughts, get out bed, and get those running clothes on as quickly as possible.

I sometimes ask myself, "Are you in control of your brain, or is your brain in control of you?" I believe we all can take control of these counterproductive thoughts and work toward those habits that bring us closer to our ultimate goals, but it takes effort. It takes intentionality.

The systems are wonderful, but, in and of themselves, they are not enough. The intentionality piece is critical. Intentionally approaching these self-care goals bolsters the systems I have built and pushes me to get out of bed and get those running clothes on. The intention comes from a regular meditation practice where I focus on my ultimate goals and hone in on what I really want out of life. With this intentional thinking as the underpinning of the systems I build, I become an unstoppable force! Intention is woven through the various facets of my life. As I set goals for the year ahead, I list the intentions behind those goals. If I set a goal to complete an Ironman triathlon later in the year, I write down *why* I want to achieve that goal. That is the intention piece. I want to achieve this goal to be a better role model for my children, to improve my health overall so I can see my grandkids grow up, etc. For me, intention is all about the purpose behind what I do, and it is literally the fuel that propels the rocket ship of success.

Is this easy to achieve? Of course not. But nothing worthwhile in life ever comes easy. Yes, it takes work, effort, and sometimes, blood, sweat, and tears. But in the end, it will certainly be worth the work.

So, what has happened to me since my decision to leave the job and implement my four foundational principles of wellness through systems and intentionality? Well, I made some significant lifestyle changes and the results have been nothing short of amazing. I lost 40 pounds in a few months' time, and I have kept it off. I weigh the same as I did when I graduated high school. My cholesterol has dropped by over 50 points without medication. I have weaned off of one of my daily medications that I was told I would be taking for the rest of my life. I have newfound energy and a zest for life that I have not felt in years. I love more, I laugh more, and I am more deeply connected to the people around me and in my life.

This state of fulfillment in life and in career do not have

to be mutually exclusive. We don't have to sacrifice one for the other. Unfortunately for me, I figured this out too late, but it doesn't have to be that way for you. That's the good news for everyone still working in this dedicated and noble profession of law enforcement. My passion in life now is to spread this good news to as many law enforcement professionals that I can to potentially save them from the same fate.

ABOUT CHIEF CHARLES CELANO (RET.)

Charlie Celano is a seasoned executive and leadership development consultant with nearly 30 years of experience in public safety. As a professional speaker, trainer, and coach, Charlie is focused on helping others, especially those in management positions, build personal and professional resilience to enhance leadership success.

Charlie spent 27 years with the Tustin Police Department in Orange County, California, working his way up through the ranks to become the 14th police chief in the department's 90-year history. Throughout his career, Charlie worked a variety of assignments, including patrol officer, field training officer, narcotics detective, gang detective sergeant, lieutenant, captain, and, ultimately, the chief of police.

Charlie is a 2014 graduate of the 258th session of the FBI National Academy for Law Enforcement Leaders. He also achieved a Bachelor of Science degree in Occupational Studies from California State University, Long Beach in 2005, and a Master of Arts degree in Business Management from the University of Redlands in 2009.

Charlie came face-to-face with his mortality in early 2018 when he was diagnosed with a serious heart condition related to chronic stress and poor lifestyle habits. After making significant changes in his life, Charlie has completely turned his health around and now shares his story of resilience and wellness in his private and public safety training to leaders all over the globe.

Most importantly, Charlie cherishes his relationships with his friends and family, especially his beautiful wife, Heidi, and his five children, Lauren, Alyssa, Chaz, Anthony, and Daniel.

Kale Won't Heal You

OFFICER ALEX MENDOZA

When we think about health, we automatically conjure up the idea of a very fit, muscular person with a pristine diet and lifestyle. At least that is what I thought when I was a young, rookie police officer first starting out.

One of my first goals was to have muscles bulging out of my uniform shirts. I worked out like a madman, ate protein every three to four hours, and carried a large water jug that looked like I was going to trek a month in the desert. I was your quintessential gym rat—grunting heavy sounds whenever I lifted those heavy weights. Thanks in part to lifting, the tailor at the uniform shop who knew how to tailor my short sleeves tightly, and the constant mental schema of machismo, I achieved my goal.

Fast-forward 27 years in my law enforcement career—after numerous altercations, an extrication from a police car with the jaws of life, seeing hundreds of dead bodies, making death notifications, having people die in my arms, and the list continues—I realized this was not ideal, optimal health and wellness.

In no time, I had become one of those police statistics: a failed marriage, divorce, and two kids divided between their parents. Compounding that was the hit to my finances in selling the family home and paying the typical spousal and child support. Later on, the cycle repeated itself with another failed and heartbreaking long-term relationship. Of course, the additional child and spousal support fees furthered complicated any new relationships; it seemed like a never-ending vortex.

My idea of health vastly changed after these experiences. I invite you to entertain the idea of mental wellness: learning how to free ourselves from stress, toxins, and the clutter that is in our mind. I know, I know what you are thinking: this guy is going to get into some hippie-dippy-touchy-feely stuff, and I don't do that. Well, what if I made the title "Tactical Wellness Survival"? After all, anything you add "tactical" to in law enforcement is accepted.

As police officers, we constantly train to learn the latest techniques and strategies with the intent of bettering ourselves with new knowledge. Our smartphones are constantly updated with operating software to fix pesky bugs or improve the operating system. Yet our brains still contain the original operating software, human being 1.0.

Where did we learn to deal with our life stressors?

Where did we learn to react to the daily stimulus from relationships?

Why did I choose to become a police officer?

I will take you along my wellness journey, with the intent of inviting you to lighten your toxic buildup. What is toxic buildup, you ask? It's all the messy, gunky negativity that slowly slithers its way into our lives. If we leave these emotional toxins unattended, they'll be stuck in our minds and our bodies and manifest themselves into disease.

Many of you may have heard the word "disease" broken up into two words: "dis," meaning "not," and "ease," meaning "absence of difficulty." Therefore, "disease" can be manifested when our bodies are not at ease. Living in this stressful environment can take a big toll on our personal well-being that can creep into other areas like work and relationships.

During my time as an officer, I saw all too many failed marriages occur for a variety of reasons. Without exploring the reasons for failure from their previous relationships, many officers hastily entered into another relationship, only to experience the same struggles with their new partner.

For the majority of us, the ideal example of a relationship came from watching our parents, which ironically, might not have been the most ideal. Yes, this sounds initially offensive, and we may push off the claim, but upon a more introspective look, as adults, we repeat the patterns and mistakes that our parents made (which we swore to never do). Of course, our parents have our best interests at heart and care for us with the best skill sets that they have, but they too were repeating the behaviors of what they saw in generations prior. While done out of the idea of love, essentially, none of us knew any better.

It isn't until difficulty hits, or some sort of ideal moment arises, that we begin to take the time to start the inner healing that is so crucial for our true growth. But most of us fiddle with distractions first.

We say we are healing, but sometimes "healing" is distractions in camouflage. Distractions can be anything—dating, drinking, shopping, or thrill-seeking pleasures. Unbeknownst to us, these distractions prevent us from truly thriving and understanding ourselves. Ultimately, we just reward ourselves with a temporary reprieve in order to not truly feel the pain that we have brought onto ourselves.

The Avocado Seed Isn't Dead, It's Just a Rebirth

I was no stranger to this cyclical pattern. In the midst of the finalization of my divorce, I quickly entered into another relationship. And I blindly repeated the same behavior from my prior marriage, which, of course, was deeply rooted in my childhood.

My parents were both from South America, so traditional gender roles ran deep: my dad, the stern, controlling disciplinarian, and my mom, the homemaker. Of course, I mimicked what I observed. Naturally, I presumed my partner would be the same way—chores and home-making skills would be second-hand by nature.

Without any self-realization, my repeated behaviors became the catalyst to my most devastating, but eye-opening journey. After seven and a half years, that relationship ended, and I was heartbroken. I truly loved this person and had envisioned being with them for the rest of my life.

While it felt like my life was over, it was truly just unfolding. Imagine looking at an avocado seed that is sprouting; the seed externally looks like it is frail and coming undone, but upon closer inspection, it is actually a rebirth.

Pain had proven to be the greatest teacher, the greatest gift. But when you are in pain, you just can't see it!

Pain Is Your Greatest Teacher

Of course, there were other invaluable gifts during this time as well. My sister became my mentor; she guided, challenged, and encouraged me to look at my own actions instead of those of others. In life, it can be so much easier to blame the other person in an effort to avoid the responsibility of our actions and contributions in a failed relationship.

It wasn't until I felt my pain that I had the opportunity to introspectively look within and realize that my behavior was exactly the same as my father's (who, likewise, was repeating the behavior of the generation prior). In an argument, my partner requested that I help around the house by cleaning, to which I retorted with a fixed mindset, "That's not my job."

If You Love a Flower, Don't Pick it

With my own teenagers, I quickly responded to their stimuli like my father did with me, ultimately creating havoc and turmoil. I had yet to realize that my children were truly their own persons, not my puppets to control. Although they had come into this world through me and were legally my children, they truly were not mine, nor were they possessions.

There is a great quote by the philosopher Osho:

"If you love a flower, don't pick it up. Because if you pick it up it dies and it ceases to be what you love. So if you love a flower, let it be. Love is not about possession. Love is about appreciation."

I have personally observed that the more someone tries to control a partner in a relationship (or a child), the more the other pulls away. As Lydia Otten says, "The more you control someone, the further away you push them. And you'll only end up getting what you desperately didn't want."

For someone in law enforcement, this concept was very foreign since my job was all about control. This led my self-inquiry: why had I chosen a career in law enforcement?

Growing up, my father was the feared, heavy-handed disciplinarian, all too eager to chase me around the house with a leather belt in hand. It was no wonder that when an opportunity arose to become a police officer, I was enormously interested in the familiar structure, discipline, and control. By adulthood, my desire to become a police officer solidified. Of course, on a subconscious level, police work was justifiable since it was an avenue that would allow me to give back to the community; I could make a difference and it provided stability, a good source of income, and benefits.

During my exploration into why I chose law enforcement, I realized that in my childhood, I lacked control; so, of course, I went into a position that inadvertently exuded power and control. In speaking to colleagues, they too shared that there was something uncontrollable in their childhoods. Some officers were abandoned by their parents who were addicted to alcohol or drugs; others had parents who were stern disciplinarians. We all lacked any sense of control and stability.

This isn't to say that I was a dastardly abused child or a victim of horrible parenting. Rather, it's just an understanding that what was absent during my early childhood was what I needed and sought out as an adult.

We Pick Our Parents as Partners

Trauma can be disorienting. Life keeps moving forward while our brains are stuck in the past. Even if a traumatic event happened years ago, it can feel like it was yesterday or happening again in the present, which can be scary and confusing. This happens because traumatic memories are stored differently and in different areas of our brains. Working through trauma can you help release those memories and regain life's footing.

A friend of mine recommended I read a book called *Getting the Love You Want*, by Harville Hendrix, PhD, and Helen Hunt, PhD.

Hendrix has worked as a relationship therapist over the last 30 years. Together with his wife, Hunt (also a therapist), they share their experiences based on psychoanalysis and scientific research. Their ultimate goal is to help transform relationships into lasting sources of love and companionship.

The first part of the book explores how we choose our partners. The unconscious mind influences our choice. Take a moment to think about the personality traits of your past and present partners.

You will discover numerous similarities between them and, surprisingly, your attention will mostly focus on their negative traits. It appears that every one of us is searching for a mate with a very specific set of positive and negative traits.

When we feel attracted to someone, we typically recognize the personality traits of our parents in that person—yes, even the negative ones. Our "old" brain thinks it has finally found the ideal candidate to make up for the psychological and emotional damage experienced in childhood. We tend to select our mates based on their resemblance to our caretakers or parents.

Hendrix and Hunt explain that people often go into a relationship hoping to heal some childhood wounds. But as much as they hope to see their partner as their parent, this is not the case.

Our "old" brain seeks to heal the wounds inflicted during our childhood, and often leads us to project negative traits on our partners. Then, as childhood traumas resurface, we expect our partner to behave in such a way that the trauma can be healed. Of course, most of the time, we don't communicate these "wounds" to our partner.

After really taking the time to digest this material, I began to understand that the partners I chose were like my father. He would not say "I love you" often, nor was he the touchy-feely type. I found myself in relationships where I wanted to fill this void, and I would literally beg my partners to express their language of love with words of affirmation or touch.

Five Ways to Understand Love

Fascinated with personal growth, I continued my journey by reading another recommended book called *The Five Love Languages*, by Gary Chapman. Chapman's conclusion is that there are five emotional love languages—five predominant ways that people speak and understand emotional love. Once we identify and learn to speak a partner's primary love language, we discover the key to a long-lasting, loving relationship.

As a society, we have been led to believe that if we are truly in love, it will last forever. However, all too many of us have experienced the harsh reality that once the euphoric feelings associated with "falling in love" have run their course, reality hits and the questions follow. Is it the right relationship? Should I stay and be miserable or jump ship?

I have experienced both—neither was a solution. Pursuing real love involves understanding your love language and that of your partner. If you and your partner share the top three love languages, understanding and expressing love will be very fluid and natural. If you do not, it will take much more effort and understanding on both parts.

I recommend reading Chapman's book and then taking the test at 5lovelanguages.com. Share and compare your results with your partner.

My results did not surprise: words of affirmation, quality time, and physical touch were tied for the top; receiving gifts followed; and acts of service ranked last.

Reflecting on previous relationships, there was one in particular where my partner had difficulty expressing their love with words (which I craved); however, they constantly portrayed acts of service. I remember feeling as if my partner did not love me, which invariably caused me to feel stress and worry about the absence of love. In reality, I simply did not resonate with the language of their love due to its unfamiliarity.

It wasn't until I read the book and took the test that I came to realize that the person did love me. In fact, their top love languages were acts of service, gifts, and physical touch, but we were failing to communicate on the same level after the honeymoon phase had dissipated.

A colleague once shared about her unmatched language of love with her husband: he craved words of affirmation, but this ranked at the bottom of her love language list. Yet, although initially foreign, after repeated practice of the giving of words of affirmation, it gradually became natural to her. These acts were not done out of obligation or to serve as a mode of comparison in the relationship, but out of love to ensure that her partner's needs were met. Reciprocally, it made her feel good, ultimately strengthening the relationship.

Poisonous Emotions

Could stress and our emotions be linked to disease?

When I was experiencing relational stress, I noticed certain discomforts in my body. Perhaps this is relatable for many of you.

Prior to the advent of modern medicine, thinkers and healers recognized the link between disease and emotion. Ancient Greek, Roman, and Indian Ayurvedic physicians have all accepted this theory. Think of the "E" in emotion standing for "energy"—energy in motion.

So, the question then is, do you want your energy to go toward healing or disease?

With the dawn of modern medicine in the Eighteenth Century, the idea that our emotions could affect our physical health became scientifically taboo. However, groundbreaking research recently completed by Dr. Esther Sternberg has illuminated the invisible threads that weave the mind and body together.

She found that there's a strong linkage between the central nervous system and the immune system: stressors negatively affect molecules that contribute to our immunity in the bloodstream. She proposed that these prolonged and repeated external stressors become stored in the brain's amygdala (region responsible for housing emotions). Over time, her studies showed that rates of immunity gradually declined. Simply put, there was a negative correlation between life stressors and functions of immunity. The main contributing variable was how the experience of the stressor was lodged in the brain.

Every moment that we exist, we experience thousands of sensations that might trigger a positive, negative, or neutral emotion. While these stimuli can be entirely neutral, perception varies per person.

The stimulus can range from a trace of perfume, a light touch, a fleeting shadow, or a strain of music, which can quickly lead to a myriad of emotional responses: happiness, sadness, or no reaction. Of course, there's also physiological responses that can accompany the emotions: palpitations, sweating, or shortness of breath.

Add to this years of neglect of our mind-body-brain connection, and it is no wonder that we are decreasing the functionality of our immune systems while catalyzing the onset of diseases.

The Road to Healing

As police officers, we're exposed to external stimuli that we internalize, which causes our own biological responses. Have you experienced situations that caused your pupils to dilate and result in tunnel vision, or caused you to breathe faster? Perhaps you have been exposed to personal emotional pain that caused you to "feel sick to your stomach." These responses are our nervous systems and stress hormones reacting to a stimulus in minutes, seconds, or even milliseconds.

Once we add our own personal pain from our past or

personal traumas on top of the daily stressors of law enforcement, we end up eventually internalizing a staggering toxic overload.

If we don't take the time to understand the mind and body connection that either heals or manifests into disease, we could literally be shaving off years of our life expectancy and stifling our physical health.

In his book, *Deadly Emotions*, Dr. Don Colbert reveals a correlation between unresolved emotional reactions and a variety of illnesses and conditions. He further explains how negative emotions contribute to disease and how we can "lighten up" to ease the discomfort of those conditions and improve our health.

Additional research (Colbert 2006; Diamond 1982; Smith et al. 2004) shows a multitude of powerful correlations linking disease and negative emotions.

- Anger and hostility are linked to hypertension and coronary heart disease.

- Resentment, bitterness, unforgiveness, and self-hatred are linked to autoimmune disorders like rheumatoid arthritis, lupus, and multiple sclerosis.

- Anxiety may manifest into irritable bowel syndrome, panic attacks, and heart palpitations.

- Repressed anger may cause tension and migraines, headaches, chronic back pain, TMJ syndrome, and fibromyalgia.

"The body is never ill or healthy, for it does no more than express messages from our consciousness," write German psychologist, Thorwald Dethlefsen, and physician, Ruediger Dahlke, in *The Healing Power of Illness*. Even though it's an odd concept to grasp—that we are not only responsible for our health, but also our illnesses—it's crucial to understand that we are the singular, most vital vehicle of change. We can create, heal, or aggravate our illnesses. After all, our reactions—just like our health—are ours. They are no less than our minds or our faces (Sacks 1999).

For those that follow conventional medicine practices, the link between self-responsibility and disease remains controversial. On the other hand, in holistic health, most individuals can accept that link without questioning.

Now, don't get me wrong. While we're all responsible for how we handle the experiences in our lives, sometimes we are dealt obstructive, challenging cards that are unavoidable—a genetic disease or being the victim of divorce or abuse. Nevertheless, far too many people use such obstacles as an excuse and, inevitably, a crutch for their behavior. In actuality, challenging life circumstances serve as teaching points and opportunities to look within.

On Mindfulness

So, how do we begin this inner work?

Simple—we need to slow down.

I know what you are thinking ... I don't have time to slow down.

Have you ever experienced either of the following situations?

You run out to your car and realize you do not have your car keys. In a rush, you quickly go back inside, frantically looking for them. Of course, you're cutting it close to an appointment time, so now you're even more stressed. Finally, you find your car keys—right where you left them—in your jacket.

Or maybe you've been looking everywhere for your sunglasses only to realize they were right on top of your head.

These situations seem routine, right? Of course! We're just getting older or forgetful. But imagine, instead of fruitlessly rushing around, that we took the time to sit in a place of awareness. If we had just slowed down, we would've located what we were looking for in far less time or prevented the situation altogether. When we add up the minutes that we spend in an unnecessary panic due to haste throughout the days, weeks, months, or years, we realize that we could have saved plenty of time had we been more aware and mindful.

I was always intrigued by the idea of meditation but initially didn't look into it. It seemed impossible to maintain a mindset that was completely silent, still, and had no thought whatsoever. Of course, this was my general belief of what meditation was supposed to be. Partway into my healing journey, I enrolled in a course called MBSR (mindfulness-based stress reduction), one of the few very well studied mindfulness programs with concrete, scientific data to support its benefits.

Jon Kabat-Zinn, PhD—scientist, writer, meditation teacher—helped bring mindfulness into mainstream medicine and society. Having received his PhD in molecular biology from MIT, with multiple awards, he discovered that mindfulness training and the practice of meditation could produce measurable biological changes. He founded the Stress Reduction Clinic at the University of Massachusetts Medical School, where he adapted Buddhist teachings on mindfulness and developed the prototype for many stress reduction and relaxation programs.

Meditation changes the physical structure of the brain. It enhances regions responsible for learning and memory processes, emotion regulation, and perspective while decreasing the amygdala, which is involved in stress responses. In clinical trials, mindfulness training also appears to suppress inflammation pathways, boost cell-mediated immunity, and slow some aspects of biological aging (Kabat-Zinn 2013).

Are you concerned that I want you to sit on the ground,

close your eyes, start to hum "Om," and try not to think about anything? That was my first impression of meditation! But I quickly learned that I was wrong.

Meditation, more specifically MBSR, is not about letting your thoughts wander. It isn't about trying to empty your mind so that you are not thinking of anything. Instead, the practice involves paying close attention to the present moment—our own thoughts, emotions, and sensations. When I attended a half-day silent retreat, no one spoke for six hours. Rather, we meditated via several techniques: walking meditation, body scan, visualization, and mindful eating.

Yes … eating can be mindful. But for most of us, it's not. We eat on autopilot! We eat because we are hungry or eating is something we have to do. For many of us, we eat while looking at our devices, completely distracted. For others, it's even a chore.

But if we eat mindfully, we chew slowly, feel the food's texture, and enable our taste buds to experience the many flavors, ultimately allowing us to appreciate what is being consumed. Our surroundings even become more vibrantly alive. After my six-hour silent retreat, I felt as if I'd been on a vacation for six months.

So go out there and search out MBSR programs. If you can't find one, there are great books for educating and immersing yourself in the practice. There are also plenty of YouTube videos with guided meditations.

And if you're thinking, "I don't have time for this," I offer to you this old Zen quote from Dr. Sukhraj Dhillon: "You should sit in meditation for 20 minutes a day, unless you're too busy, then you should sit for an hour."

Speaking with Kindness

How do you speak to yourself? What are the words you use toward yourself? Are they kind and nurturing? People often tell me that the words they speak to themselves are horrible. It usually sounds like:

- "I'm not good enough."
- "Why am I in this situation again?"
- "This always happens to me."
- "I'm an idiot."

After studying mindfulness, self-compassion became my next healing modality. Self-compassion is a meditation practice where you learn to speak with kindness to yourself—when you are having a difficult time, fail, or notice something you don't like about yourself. It's treating yourself how you would treat your best friend if they were experiencing hardships.

Instead of just ignoring your pain with a "suck it up" mentality, you pause and tell yourself, "This is really hard right now." You ask, "How can I comfort and care for myself in this moment?"

Once you understand the basics of meditation, I invite you to explore the practice of self-compassion meditations. The words of this empowering, soothing, and transformational type of meditation ranges:

- "May I be free of worry."
- "May I speak kind words to myself."
- "Other people have gone through this."
- "May I love and accept myself just as I am."

During one of my self-compassion courses, there was a 65-year-old woman who had recently lost her husband and was having a rough time adjusting to life without him. When our teacher asked how we were feeling after a guided meditation, her hand shot up. She said she didn't realize she could give herself permission to love, accept herself, and to speak with kindness. Many of us echoed her sentiment, which elicited a huge wake-up call for me: most of us probably don't accept ourselves how we are, nor do we give ourselves the kindness that we offer to others.

When I was asked to contribute to this book, I had planned to contribute a lot about nutrition and diet—to help you physically mitigate stress.

But in my opinion, the truth of the matter is that mental and emotional toxins are equally, if not more, destructive than the physical toxins that we eat and drink. You can have the cleanest diet and the best workout, but in the end, kale alone won't heal you. Your mental well-being is critical in obtaining optimal health.

Kale Won't Heal You

Now that we've discussed many emotional paths to wellness, it's time to delve into some physical paths. I am not here to challenge your belief system, but merely to present an invitation to explore an idea and perhaps a different lifestyle.

Some people call the way we eat a diet. But I don't like to call it that. Normally diets have a start date and an end date. For me, what worked was a "lifestyle change."

My lifestyle change was the result of food poisoning. For five days, I couldn't maintain any food in my body. After I was admitted to the hospital, I spent five more days being handed off from one doctor to another.

No one really had any idea of what was going on until finally one doctor diagnosed that I had food poisoning. I told him I had eaten marinated ceviche, shrimp in lime juice; he responded with a simple question of whether I would eat a cockroach.

Easy response for me: "Absolutely not!" The doctor then said, "Shrimp is the cockroach of the sea." He told me the most commonly admitted patients with food poisoning have consumed either shrimp or chicken.

Nonchalantly, he ordered me some food and guaranteed that as long as I could keep it in me, that I was considered cured and could just follow up with my regular physician.

The food tray arrived with a ham and cheese sandwich on white bread, potato chips, apple juice concentrate, stale carrot sticks, and Jell-O.

With a quick glance, the thoughts came swirling: "Good grief! Is this really food? Who is in charge of my nutrition—that guy in the white lab coat that just came in (who doesn't even look that healthy)? Where does my food come from? How is it grown? What did they feed my food?"

Naturally, my investigative skills kicked in and I immersed myself in several documentaries to discover the relationships to where my food comes from. I discovered that marketing plays a key role in the portrayal of food, which is often far from how we envision chickens, cows, and other animals that our meats come from. In the supermarkets or in commercials, we always see cows in green pastures or chickens roaming freely. Once I discovered the real truth, I was shocked.

My biggest eye-opening experience came from reading the book, *The China Study*, by T. Colin Campbell, PhD, Professor Emeritus of Nutritional Biochemistry at Cornell University, and his son, Dr. Thomas M. Campbell II. The elder Dr. Campbell conducted a 20-year study that was described by the *New York Times* as "the Grand Prix of Epidemiology." He examined the link between the consumption of animal products (including dairy) and chronic illnesses like cancer, heart disease, and diabetes.

His research on the causation of diseases and the correlation of consuming animal products and the onset of disease astonished me. Dr. Campbell did not approach his research with a bias (he grew up on a dairy farm); he was a scientist doing research. Furthermore, Dr. Campbell does not categorize himself as vegan; instead, he identifies as being a whole foods plant-based eater.

Nobel Prize winner Elizabeth Blackburn found that a vegan diet caused more than 500 or so genes to change within three months. Not only does a vegan diet activate genes that counteract diseases, but it also turns off genes that cause breast cancer, heart disease, prostate cancer, and other illnesses. Dr. Dean Ornish, who developed the Ornish Diet, showed that heart disease is reversible by making diet and lifestyle changes including healthy dieting, stress management, exercise, and social support. Many researchers have concluded that our diets are the singular most effective element in changing the length of our telomeres.

Telomeres are often compared to the plastic tips on the ends of shoelaces. Their job is to stop the ends of the chromosomes from fraying or sticking together. Telomeres play an important role in making sure our DNA is copied correctly when a cell divides. When DNA is damaged, the end of the telomere shortens as it begins to unravel. At a critical length, telomere shortening can trigger aging and cause a shorter life span (Shammas 2011; Whittemore et al. 2019).

Additionally, in a TED Talk, Assistant Professor of Anthropology at Harvard University Christina Warinner explained that humans actually have "no known anatomical, physiological, or genetic adaptations to meat consumption." In fact, humans actually have many adaptations for plant eating. There are plenty of paleoanthropologists that show that our ancestors ate nuts, tubers, plantains, water chestnuts, and, only occasionally, some meat.

In light of these studies, you may be wondering about the popularity of the paleo diet, which is based on what our ancestors ate. It includes plants, meat, fish, and fresh fruit and vegetables. It avoids any food that is cultivated only via farming, including grains, dairy, and even legumes such as lentils and beans. I don't believe that the paleo diet is the answer. First, it doesn't take into account that the food our ancestors would have eaten depended greatly on the area they lived in—its geographical location, seasons, and climate. Second, just because it might have worked for our ancestors doesn't make it the right fit now. After all, they also did without cars, tv, and cell phones!

And most important, recent studies on animal products show that they're not the optimal proteins that paleo diet supporters might think that they are.

The World Health Organization considers processed meats carcinogenic to humans. Processed meat has been given a Group 1 classification, putting it in the same class of cancer risk as tobacco smoking and asbestos.

Red meat has been categorized as a Group 2A carcinogen, which means it is "probably carcinogenic to humans." It's the same classification assigned to the pesticide glyphosate.

Animal products including meat (along with dairy) are the main dietary sources of saturated fats. According to the American Heart Association, eating foods that contain these fats raises cholesterol levels. High levels of cholesterol increase the risk of heart disease and stroke.

Beyond the animal products themselves, you are consuming any pharmaceutical drugs injected into them. Furthermore, you have to consider your ingestion of the herbicides, pesticides, fungicides, and insecticides that have been placed into the feed of the animals you consume. You know what else ends with the "cide"? Suicide—no thank you!

Well, what about fish?

Did you know that fish have been tested and have been found to contain microplastics? These microplastics affect your hormones and have other health consequences. Oh, but what about those omega-3s? The majority of those oils are rancid oils, which can accelerate the aging process and lead to other health problems. Do you want a good source of omega-3s? Try purslane, a weed that most people pull from their landscape. Purslane contains more omega-3 fatty acids than some fish. In fact, there are many varieties of plant-based omega-3 sources, such as chia seeds, flax, and clary sage oil.

How about eggs?

Nope. Do not believe the marketing. Did you know the American Egg Board is a promotional marketing board appointed by the U.S. government? Their mission is to "increase demand for egg and egg products on behalf of U.S. egg producers."

Dr. Michael Greger discovered that the head of the USDA's poultry research and promotion programs has reminded egg companies that eggs and egg products cannot be classified as being healthy or nutritious. Per the USDA: "The words 'nutritious' and 'healthy' carry certain connotations, and because eggs have the amount of cholesterol that they do, plus the fact that they're not low in fat, [the words healthy and nutritious] are problematic."

When told that they couldn't use "Nutritional powerhouse" either, the American Egg Board proposed the ad headline: "Egg-ceptional Nutrition." But they couldn't say that because, again, given the saturated fat and cholesterol, eggs legally couldn't be called nutritious. So the headline ended up as, "Find true satisfaction," and instead of weight loss, they had to claim eggs "can reduce hunger." The USDA congratulated them on their cleverness. Yes, a food that when eaten can reduce hunger—what a concept!

Are there any benefits from dairy?

No! Have you ever questioned the purpose of cow's milk? It turns a 65-pound calf into a 400-pound cow as rapidly as possible. In cow's milk, there are naturally occurring hormones, pus, lipids, proteins, sodium, and IGF-1 (insulin-like growth factor). All of that is designed to blow up that calf into a great big cow. Cow's milk is the lactation secretions of a large mammal that just had a baby cow. Look at yourself in the mirror—do you see a tail or big ears?

The only time humans need IGF-1 is when we are babies—hence the name "growth factor." IGF-1 is necessary for proper growth in children. Once mother's milk is not available, you are not supposed to have it anymore! If IGF-1's job is to trigger growth and you consume it, could it cause something inside of you to grow? Researchers from Harvard Medical School have stated that high levels of growth factor can significantly increase the risks of colorectal, breast, and prostate cancer. IGF-1 can activate or promote pathways in cancer cells.

If you feel like you need milk with your cereal (a denatured food that you should not be eating), then find a good plant-based milk without all the gums. Better yet, check on YouTube for how to make almond milk, coconut milk, or oat milk. It's easy and much better!

Of course, anything and everything one believes can be supported or argued against by merely searching about it online—even my own beliefs about the negatives of animal products. But what truly sold me was 60 years' worth of scientific research that Dr. Campbell did. No one can touch that!

I too support and live and whole foods plant-based life-style. This lifestyle is more than just veganism. Sometimes veganism can be unhealthy. Overly-processed "meats" are not healthy foods; neither is vegan pizza slathered with cheese made from various binding gums. I call these transitional foods; they're designed to help those that are moving toward a plant-based lifestyle. Ultimately, the more whole foods you consume, the better your health will be! I would gladly have a black bean and quinoa burger, lettuce-wrapped, of course!

The more I have researched, the more I have discovered that a strong plant-based lifestyle is associated with better health and longevity.

Many areas of the world where there is little disease and longer life spans (called Blue Zones) have more centenarians who eat mainly plant-based whole foods. Okinawa, Japan, alone has 68 centenarians; this is more than three times the numbers found in U.S. populations of the same size. The majority of their dietary consumption is approximately 96 percent plant-based. In Loma Linda California, the Seventh Day Adventists live as much as a decade longer as the rest of the population, and they eat a vegan or vegetarian diet.

The Physicians Committee for Responsible Medicine (PCRM) is an organization of 12,000 doctors that recommend and advocate for a plant-based lifestyle. They have a food plate recommendation of legumes, fruit, vegetables, and grains. Note their name: "Physicians

Committee for Responsible Medicine." These folks believe you should be getting your daily nutrients from the "Farmacy" not the "pharmacy"!

The producers of the documentary, *Game Changers*, highlight the world's strongest man, Patrik Baboumian, as he flips a car while documenting his vegan diet. NFL players, MLB players, UFC fighters, and other athletes have gone plant-based and touted the increased energy and recovery benefits.

You may wonder how to get protein in a whole foods plant-based lifestyle. We really do not need a lot of protein. For example, the perfect food for an infant is mother's milk, which actually contains less than 3 percent protein! Yet it is the perfect food for life, providing enough nourishment for growth. Broccoli contains more protein per calorie than steak and, per calorie, spinach is about equal to chicken and fish. It's not tricky to get a sustainable amount of protein.

Oh, wait! I can hear some of you saying, "I've heard that legumes and other vegetables contain lectins (proteins that can bind to carbohydrates), which are not good for you." Throughout history, ancient civilizations have consumed legumes and other lectin-containing vegetables. In 1963, researchers at Massachusetts General conducted a study where plant lectins were found to almost completely suppress the growth of human head and neck cancer cells, liver cancer cells, and breast cancer cells within three days.

Bottom line: When researching a lifestyle change for optimal health and nutrition, look at the science—the real science where no one is gaining financially. Do not get suckered into the latest fad book complete with a line of powders and vitamins you can take that the author is selling. Be aware that some of the keto and paleo information is funded by the meat industry—shocker that they would have an interest.

These diets are great marketing! They help convince us to eliminate processed foods, breads, and dairy—all of which we should not be eating anyway—yet allow us to eat the same inflammatory foods. If you strive for a long, healthy life, getting your protein from beans, nuts, and grains is a much better bet than getting it from animal products.

Today, more than ever, it's easy to transition to a plant-based lifestyle. Don't fall into the trap of telling yourself, "I couldn't go plant-based. It's too hard."

Choose your words carefully. How about replacing "It's too hard," with "I can do it—it will just be different!" This is exponentially more empowering.

Whichever lifestyle trajectory you choose in an effort to reduce your universally-felt stress, be sure to choose personal growth as the ultimate goal. Remember, mental and emotional toxins are equally, if not more, destructive than physical toxins.

It takes more than kale alone to heal.

May you mindfully eat, rest, live, and love.

ABOUT OFFICER ALEX MENDOZA

Alex is a passionate public speaker and ambassador for the plant-based eating movement. He has been a police officer for over 28 years. He is divorced and has two adult kids. He earned his certificate in Plant-Based Nutrition through the T. Colin Campbell Center for Nutrition Studies, Cornell University. The curriculum was developed by one of the most knowledgeable, experienced, and respected physicians advocating for plant-based nutrition, Dr. T. Colin Campbell, Professor Emeritus, Cornell University.

Alex presents a new paradigm for nutrition, one rooted in evidenced-based research in order to enable people to prevent, reverse, and battle chronic, degenerative disease, and achieve optimal health through a proper lifestyle of plant-based whole food, self-compassion, meditation, and emotional intelligence. Alex is an avid meditation practitioner and holds a Reiki Level II certificate.

Helping people learn the links between the mind-body connection, stress prevention, diet and disease, and the transformative powers of disease prevention is his passion.

Final Thoughts

KATHRYN HAMEL, PhD

In writing *Body, Mind, and Badge: Strategies for Navigating Trauma and Resilience in Law Enforcement*, it was my desire to bring together thought leaders in their respective fields and to integrate their collective wisdom into one easy to follow road map to law enforcement resiliency. Along the way, I shared my journey to physical fitness and wellness while my colleagues shared their best practices for healing, holistic health, nutrition, wellness, and resiliency. Whether or not you choose to follow our road map or use it as a starting point for your own, we are pleased to start the conversation.

While this conversation is all too often left to the midpoint or end of one's career, we encourage you to start it now—whether you are at day one, week one, or year five or twenty-five. We honor your commitment to the profession of policing and law enforcement. We desire for you to get to other side of your career despite the darkness, sadness, and isolation that sometimes accompanies the profession and the responsibility borne by law enforcement officers.

Start taking care of yourself—your mind and your body—because in these turbulent times, you are called upon more so than ever to be peacemaker, counselor, and shoulder to cry on, all the while being warrior, peace officer, and law enforcer. And yet, you are so much more than even these roles, and you owe it to yourselves, your peers, your family, your friends, your departments, and your communities to be the best version of yourself—most of the time. There will be moments when you may turn to the comfort of food, alcohol, gambling, or exercise—all things in moderation.

Strive for the adaptive coping mechanisms, not the maladaptive ones. Why? Because you owe it to the present and future version of yourself. Take the time to process the critical events, the suicides, the death, the horrific crimes committed against our most vulnerable populations. Do not let these moments define you, for you will find yourself in the darkest of places. Instead, find the moments of camaraderie, bravery, and joy. And most of all celebrate each day that you find yourself wishing to be the best, most resilient version of yourself.

Someone once told me that your view of the organization depends on your seat in the organization. For those with a seat of influence, I encourage you to embrace physical fitness and wellness programs for your organizations. Embrace self-care, resiliency, physical fitness, mindfulness, and wellness for yourselves and your officers. I encourage you to explore options for program incentives. From a fiscal perspective, the value of these programs cannot be overstated. It is my assertion that healthier, happier, and more engaged officers take less time off, are not injured as often, and utilize less sick time resulting in decreased costs overall. Engaged officers also receive fewer complaints from the public. In all, resilient officers better serve their respective communities.

You have been offered words of wisdom, advice, and reflections from law enforcement officers at every level—front line, supervisory, and management. With each page we populated with our words, our stories, and our journeys, we sincerely hope that our lessons help you become resilient and cultivate staff resilience within your ranks when possible. We need you now more than ever ... be resilient, stay focused, and be engaged no matter where you are in your career! Be well and stay safe!

WORKS CITED

"Hey! You're Gonna Go Through a Whole Change in Your Entire Life" Insights for Navigating Shift Work

DWI Detection and Standardized Field Sobriety Testing (SFST). National Highway Traffic Safety Administration, Oct. 2015.

Romas, J. A., and M. Sharma. *Practical Stress Management: A Comprehensive Workbook for Managing Change and Promoting Health.* 7th ed., Academic Press, 2017.

Samuels, C. "Ways to Avoid Sleep Deprivation." *National Institute of Justice Journal*, no. 262, Mar. 2009, p. 31.

Vila, B. "Sleep Deprivation: What Does It Mean for Public Safety Officers?" *National Institute of Justice Journal*, no. 262, Mar. 2009, pp. 26–30.

Impact of Physical Fitness on Law Enforcement Officer Stress and Coping Skills

Aaron, J. D. "Stress and coping in police officers." *Police Quarterly*, vol. 3, no. 4, Dec. 2000, pp. 438–50, DOI: 10.1177/1098611110000300405.

Barling, J., et al., editors. *Handbook of work stress.* Thousand Oaks, CA, SAGE, 2005.

Baughman, P., et al. "Central Adiposity and Subclinical Cardiovascular Disease in Police Officers." *ISRN Obesity*, vol. 2013, DOI: 10.1155/2013/895687.

Becker, C., et al. "Law enforcement preferences for PTSD treatment and crisis management alternatives." *Behavior Research and Therapy*, vol. 47, no. 3, Mar. 2009, pp. 245–53, DOI: 10.1016/j.brat.2009.01.001.

Benavides, A. D., and H. David. "Local government wellness programs: A viable option to decrease healthcare costs and improve productivity." *Public Personnel Management*, vol. 39, no. 4, 2010, pp. 291–306.

Bullock, T. (n.d.). "Police officer injury study." VML Insurance Programs, www.vmlins.org/Newsletters/Law/injury.htm.

Chae, M. H., and D. J. Boyle. "Police suicide: Prevalence, risk, and protective factors." *Policing: An International Journal*, vol. 36, no. 1, Mar. 2013, pp. 91–118, DOI: 10.1108/13639511311302498.

Collingwood, T. R., et al. "The need for physical fitness." *Law and Order*, vol. 3, 2004, pp. 44–50.

Dugdill, L., et al. *Physical activity and health promotion: Evidence based approaches to practice*. Chichester, UK, Wiley-Blackwell, 2009.

Fiedler, M. L. *Officer safety and wellness: An overview of the issues*. Community Oriented Policing Services, USDOJ, 2009, cops.usdoj.gov/pdf/OSWG/e091120401-OSWGReport.pdf.

Galatzer-Levy, I. R., et al. "Peritraumatic and trait dissociation differentiate police officers with resilient versus symptomatic trajectories of posttraumatic stress symptoms." *Journal of*

Traumatic Stress, vol. 24, no. 5, 2011, pp. 557–65, DOI: 10.1002/jts.20684.

Gerber, M., et al. "Do exercise and fitness buffer against stress among Swiss police and emergency response service officers?" *Psychology of Sport and Exercise*, vol. 11, no. 4, July 2010, pp. 284–94, DOI: 10.1016/j.psychsport.2010.02.004.

Gilmartin, K.M. *Emotional Survival for Law Enforcement: A Guide for Officers and Their Families*. Tucson, AZ, E-S Press, 2002.

Halpern, J., et al. "Interventions for critical incident stress in emergency medical services: A qualitative study." *Stress & Health: Journal of the International Society for the Investigation of Stress*, vol. 25, no. 2, Oct. 2008, pp. 139–49, DOI: 10.1002/smi.1230.

Harris, K. W. "Increasing mental fitness." *The Futurist*, vol. 43, no. 3, 2009, pp. 53–54.

Johnson, R. "Officer fitness." *Law & Order*, vol. 57, no. 1, 2009, p. 18.

Kasper, J. "Comprehensive wellness programs: Maintaining physical and mental fitness." *Law & Order*, vol. 58, no. 11, 2010, pp. 70–73.

Lagestad, P. "Physical Skills and Work Performance in Policing." *International Journal of Police Science & Management*, vol. 14, no. 1, Mar. 2012, pp. 58–70, DOI: 10.1350/ijps.2012.14.1.259.

Morash, M., et al. "Multilevel influences on police stress." *Journal of Contemporary Criminal Justice*, vol. 22, no. 1, Feb. 2006, pp. 26–43, DOI: 10.1177/1043986205285055.

Novy, M. "Cognitive distortions during law enforcement shooting." *Activitas Nervosa Superior*, vol. 54, no. 1, 2012, pp. 60–66.

Parks, K. M., and L. A. Steelman. "Organizational wellness programs: A meta-analysis." *Journal of Occupational Health Psychology*, vol. 13, no. 1, Jan. 2008, pp. 58–68. DOI: 10.1037/1076-8998.13.1.58.

Quigley, A. "Fit for duty? The need for physical fitness programs for law enforcement officers." *The Police Chief*, vol. 75, no. 6, 2008, pp. 62–64.

Regehr, C., et al. "Acute stress and performance in police recruits." *Stress and Health*, vol. 24, no. 4, July 2008, pp. 295–303. DOI: 10.1002/smi.1182.

Smith, J. E., and G. G. Tooker. *Health and fitness in law enforcement: A voluntary model program response to a critical issue.* CALEA, no. 87, Feb. 2005, www.tacticalfunctionaltraining.com/Content/images/HealthandFitnessinLawEnforcement.pdf.

Tanigoshi, H., et al. "The effectiveness of individual wellness counseling on the wellness of law enforcement officers." *Journal of Counseling & Development*, vol. 86, no. 1, Dec. 2008, pp. 64–74, DOI: 10.1002/j.1556-6678.2008.tb00627.x.

Violanti, J. M., et al. "The Buffalo cardio-metabolic occupational police stress (BCOPS) pilot study: Design, methods and measurement." *Annals of Epidemiology*, vol. 16, 2006, pp. 148–56.

Violanti, J. M., et al. *On the edge: Recent perspectives on police suicide*. Springfield, IL, Thomas, 2011.

Violanti, J. M., et al. "Shift work and long-term injury among police officers." *Scandinavian Journal of Work, Environment & Health*, vol. 39, no. 4, July 2013, pp. 361–68, DOI: 10.5271/ sjweh.3342.

Wall, C. L., et al. "The workers' compensation experience: A qualitative exploration of workers' beliefs regarding the impact of the compensation system on their recovery and rehabilitation. *International Journal of Disability Management*, vol. 4, no. 2, Sept. 2009, pp. 19–26, DOI: 10.1375/jdmr.4.2.19.

Wirth, M., et al. "Shiftwork duration and the awakening cortisol response among police officers." *Chronobiology International: The Journal of Biological & Medical Rhythm Research*, vol. 28, no. 5, 2011, pp. 446–57, DOI: 10.3109/07420528.2011.573112.

Yuan, C., et al. "Protective factors for post-traumatic stress disorder symptoms in a prospective study of police officers." *Psychiatry Research*, vol. 188, no. 4, 2011.

Predictive Injury Testing, Biomechanics, and Corrective
Exercise: One Component of Officer Wellness

Bates, G., et al. "Core strength: A new model for injury
prediction and prevention." *Journal of Occupational Medicine
and Toxicology*, vol. 2, no. 3, 2007, DOI: 10.1186/1745-6673-2-3.
Accessed 1 Dec. 2012.

Benjaminse, A., et al. "Which Screening Tools Can Predict
Injury to the Lower Extremities in Team Sports?" *Sports
Medicine*, vol. 42, no. 9, 2012, pp. 791–815, DOI:
dx.doi.org/10.2165/11632730-000000000-00000. Accessed 27
Jan. 2013.

Brosseau, C. "Injuries to cops, firefighters, cost $20M since
'02." *Tucson Citizen*, 10 Sept. 2008. Accessed 1 Dec. 2012.

Bullock, T. (n.d.). "Police officer injury study." VML Insurance
Programs,www.vmlins.org/Newsletters/Law/injury.htm.
Accessed 21 Feb. 2012.

Cassidy, J. "Fire, police rack up workers' comp." *The Orange
County Register*, 17 Sept. 2011, www.ocregister.com/articles/
claims-317704-city-workers.html. Accessed 18 Mar. 2012.

Ceniceros, R. "Wellness program seeks to reduce police
workers comp claims." *Business Insurance*, 20 Nov. 2001, www.
businessinsurance.com/article/20111120/NEWS08/311209980.
Accessed 21 Mar. 2012.

Contreras, M. "The Performance and Financial Benefits of Using the Functional Movement Screen in the Fire Service." Orange County Fire Authority, 2010 (unpublished manuscript).

Contreras, M. In-person interview, 18 Jan. 2013, Irvine, CA.

Cook, G., et al. *The Functional Movement Screen and Exercise Progressions Manual*, functionalmovement.com. Accessed 16 Nov. 2012.

Filipa, A., et al. "Neuromuscular Training Improves Performance on the Star Excursion Balance Test in Young Female Athletes." *Journal of Orthopaedic & Sports Physical Therapy*, vol. 40, no. 9, 2010, pp. 551–58, DOI: 10.2519/jospt.2010.3325. Accessed 6 Feb. 2013.

Hagger, M. S., and N. Chatzisarantis. "Transferring motivation from educational to extramural contexts: a review of the trans-contextual model." *European Journal of Psychology of Education*, vol. 27, no. 2, 2012, pp. 195–212, DOI: 10.1007/s10212-011-0082-5. Accessed 8 Dec. 2012.

Krainik, P. W. "Up Close: Physical Standards." *Law and Order*, vol. 5, no. 3, 2003, pp. 54–57. Accessed 25 Nov. 2012.

Langston, D. Telephone conversation, 15 Feb. 2013.

Mefferd, K. Telephone conversation, 28 Jan. 2013.

Lisman, P., et al. "Functional Movement Screen and Aerobic Fitness Predict Injuries in Military Training." *Medicine*

& *Science in Sports & Exercise*, 27 Nov. 2012, DOI: 10.1249/ MSS.0b013e31827a1c4c. Accessed 5 Feb. 2013.

Schneiders, A. G., et al. "Functional Movement Screen Normative Values in a Young, Active Population." *The International Journal of Sports Physical Therapy*, vol. 6, no. 2, 2011, pp. 75–82, www.researchgate.net/publication/51452094_ Functional_Movement_Screen_Normative_values_in_a_ young_active_population. Accessed 26 Jan. 2013.

Steinhardt, M., et al. "The Relationship of Physical Activity and Cardiovascular Fitness to Absenteeism and Medical Care Claims Among Law Enforcement Officers." *American Journal of Health Promotion*, vol. 5, no. 6, 1991, pp. 455–60, DOI: dx. doi.org/10.4278/0890-1171-5.6.455. Accessed 7 Dec. 2012.

Stevens, H. Telephone conversation, 14 Feb. 2013.

Wann, T. Telephone conversation, 4 Feb. 2013.

Cultivating Resiliency in Law Enforcement

Andersen, J. P., et al. "Applying Resilience Promotion Training Among Special Forces Police Officers." *SAGE Open*, vol. 5, no. 2, Apr. 2015, DOI: doi.org/10.1177/2158244015590446.

Arnetz, B. B., et al. "Trauma Resilience Training for Police: Psychophysiological and Performance Effects." *Journal of Police and Criminal Psychology*, vol. 24, Apr. 2009, pp. 1–9, DOI: doi.org/10.1007/s11896-008-9030-y.

Arnetz, B. B., and E. Arble. "First responder stress, resilience, and performance: A national study across first responder groups." *The 10th International Conference on Occupational Stress and Health, May 16–19, 2013, Los Angeles, California: Protecting and Promoting Total Worker Health [Abstracts]*, DOI: 10.1037/e577572014-179.

Backman, L., et al. "Psychophysiological effects of mental imaging training for police trainees." *Stress Medicine*, vol. 13, no. 1, Jan. 1997, pp. 43–48; DOI: 10.1002/(SICI)1099-1700(199701)13:1<43::AID-SMI716>3.0.CO;2-6.

Brooks, S. K., et al. "Social and occupational factors associated with psychological distress and disorder among disaster responders: A systematic review." *BMC Psychology*, 4, 2016, DOI: http://dx.doi.org.proxy1.calsouthern.edu/10.1186/s40359-016-0120-9.

Chae, M. H., and D. J. Boyle. "Police suicide: prevalence, risk, and protective factors." *Policing: An International Journal of Police Strategies & Management*, vol. 36, no. 1, 2013, pp. 91–118, DOI: 10.1108/13639511311302498.

Collier, L. "Growth after trauma." *Monitor on Psychology*, vol. 47, no. 10, Nov. 2016, www.apa.org/monitor/2016/11/growth-trauma.

Evans, R., et al. "Police officers' experiences of supportive and unsupportive social interactions following traumatic incidents." *European Journal of Psychotraumatology*, 4, 2013, DOI: 10.3402/ejpt.v4i0.19696.

Goerling, R. "Officer safety corner: The role of mindfulness training in policing a democratic society." *The Police Chief*, vol. LXXXI, no. 4, Apr. 2014, static1.squarespace.com/static/54ffab2ee4b0126b07f8a557/t/555169b0e4b0471a8409dc6f/1431398832098/Police+Chief+Magazine+-+APR14.pdf.

Herndon, J. (n.d). "Police stress, psychological debriefing and organizational climate: An empirical study of intervention effectiveness." *Police Stress, Psychological Debriefing and Organizational Climate: An Empirical Study of Intervention Effectiveness*, 1, DOI: 10.1037/e338022004-001.

Hesketh, I. "Well-being, Austerity and Policing: Is it worth it to invest in resiliency training?" *Police Journal: Theory, Practice and Principles*, vol. 88, no. 3, 2014, pp. 220–30, DOI: 10.1177/0032258X15598950.

Karaffa, K. M., and R. R. Thrasher. "Revisiting Stress." *The Police Chief*, May 2016, pp. 26–32, www.policechiefmagazine.org/revisiting-stress.

Miller, L. "Law Enforcement Traumatic Stress: Clinical Syndromes and Intervention Strategies." *American Academy of Experts in Traumatic Stress, Inc.*, 1999, ovc.ojp.gov/sites/g/files/xyckuh226/files/media/document/ci_police_stress_and_interventions-508.pdf; also available at www.aaets.org/article87.htm.

Miller, L. "Police Officer Stress: Syndromes and Strategies for Intervention." *Behind the Badge*. Routledge, 2014.

Nicoletti, J., et al. "Supporting the Psychological Recovery of First Responders Following a Mass Casualty Event." *The Police Chief*, 83, June 2016, pp. 40–45, www.policechiefmagazine. org/supporting-the-psychological-recovery.

Papazoglou, K. "Conceptualizing Police Complex Spiral Trauma and its Applications in the Police Field." *Traumatology*, vol. 19, no. 3, 2012, pp. 196–209, DOI: 10.1177/153465612466151.

Papazoglou, K., and J. P. Andersen. "A guide to utilizing police training as a tool to promote resilience and improve health outcomes among police officers." *Traumatology: An International Journal*, vol. 20, no. 2, 2014, pp. 103–111, DOI: 10.1037/h0099394.

Paton, D., et al. "Disaster response: risk, vulnerability and resilience." *Disaster Prevention and Management*, vol. 9, no. 3, 2000, pp. 173–180, DOI: doi.org/10.1108/09653560010335068.

Paton, D. "Critical incident stress risk in police officers: Managing resilience and vulnerability." *Traumatology*, vol. 12, no. 3, 2006, pp. 198–206, DOI: doi.org/10.1177/1534765606296532.

Paton, D., and K. Burke. "Personal and organizational predictors of posttraumatic adaptation and growth in police officers." *Australasian Journal of Disaster and Trauma Studies*, vol. 2007 (1), 2007.

Shakespeare-Finch, J., et al. "Social support, self-efficacy, trauma, and well-being in emergency medical dispatchers." *Social Indicators Research*, 123, 2015, pp. 549–65, DOI: 10.1037/e590292013-001.

Southwick, S. M., et al. "Resilience: An Update." *PTSD Research Quarterly*, vol. 25, no. 4, 2015.

Techmanski, M. "Critical Incident Stress Management and Peer Support for Law Enforcement Personnel: An Objective Review of Data and Practice for Administrators." *The Journal of Law Enforcement*, vol. 3, no. 2, 2014.

Yuan, C., et al. "Protective factors for post-traumatic stress disorder symptoms in a prospective study of police officers." *Psychiatry Research*, vol. 188, no. 4, 2011.

Kale Won't Heal You

Campbell, T. C., and T. M. Campbell II. *The China Study*. Dallas, BenBella Books, Inc., 2016.

Chapman, G. *The Five Love Languages*. Chicago, Northfield Publishing, 2015.

Colbert, D. *Deadly Emotions*. Nashville, Emanate Books, 2006.

Dethlefsen, T., and R. Dahlke. *The Healing Power of Illness*. Sentient Publications, 2016.

Diamond, E. L. "The role of anger and hostility in essential hypertension and coronary heart disease." *Psychological Bulletin*, vol. 92, no. 2, 1982, pp. 410–33, DOI: doi.org /10.1037/0033-2909.92.2.410.

Hendrix, H., and H. Hunt. *Getting the Love You Want*. New York, St. Martin's Griffin, 2019.

Kabat-Zinn, J. *Full Catastrophe Living: Using the Wisdom of Your Body and Mind to Face Stress, Pain, and Illness*. New York, Bantam Books, 2013.

Sacks, O. *Awakenings*. New York, Vintage Books, 1999.

Shammas, M. A. "Telomeres, lifestyle, cancer, and aging." *Current Opinion in Clinical Nutrition and Metabolic Care*, vol. 14, no. 1, Jan. 2011, pp. 28–34, DOI: 10.1097/MCO.0b013e32834121b1.

Smith, T., et al. "Hostility, Anger, Aggressiveness, and Coronary Heart Disease: An Interpersonal Perspective on Personality, Emotion, and Health." *Journal of Personality*, Oct. 2004, DOI: doi.org/10.1111/j.1467-6494.2004.00296.x.

Whittemore, K., et al. "Telomere shortening rate predicts species life span." *PNAS*, vol. 116, no. 30, July 2019, pp. 15122–27; DOI: doi.org/10.1073/pnas.1902452116.